The **OFFICIAL** *HISTORY* *of* **BRITAIN**

The OFFICIAL *HISTORY of* BRITAIN

**Our story in numbers as told by the
Office for National Statistics**

BORIS STARLING
with DAVID BRADBURY

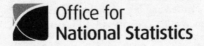

Office for
National Statistics

HarperCollins*Publishers*

HarperCollins*Publishers*
1 London Bridge Street
London SE1 9GF

www.harpercollins.co.uk

HarperCollins*Publishers*
1st Floor, Watermarque Building, Ringsend Road
Dublin 4, Ireland

First published by HarperCollins*Publishers* 2020
This revised and updated edition published 2022

1 3 5 7 9 10 8 6 4 2

A catalogue record of this book is
available from the British Library

ISBN 978-0-00-841222-7

Printed and bound in the UK using 100%
renewable electricity at CPI Group (UK) Ltd

MIX
Paper from
responsible sources
FSC™ C007454

This book is produced from independently certified FSC™ paper
to ensure responsible forest management.

For more information visit: www.harpercollins.co.uk/green

CONTENTS

FOREWORD TO THE PAPERBACK EDITION

by Professor Sir Ian Diamond, UK National Statistician

When I wrote the foreword to the hardback edition of this book we were only a few months into a global pandemic, but it was already clear how vital it was to have good data to underpin the national response to the coronavirus outbreak. Indeed, I'd suggest that never before this outbreak had statistics been so crucial in informing the decisions that affect us all. As COVID-19 has continued since then to affect our daily lives, we in the Office for National Statistics have carried on producing some of the key numbers that have informed this response. There's a reason it matters, summed up by the great scientist Lord Kelvin, who once said that 'if you cannot measure it, you cannot improve it.'

Britain has a long tradition of measuring things about the life of the country with a view to improving them. True, William the Conqueror commissioned the Domesday Book to tax his realm rather than improve it, but the publication of regular bills of mortality in Tudor and Stuart London allowed the authorities to track outbreaks of infection and take precautions. Subsequently, the nineteenth century saw great strides in official data – for example the decennial census from 1801 onwards, originally designed to monitor whether the population was growing or shrinking, and then the registration of births, marriages and deaths to provide comprehensive national data. Florence Nightingale, as well as championing professional standards in nursing, was also a pioneer in the presentation of statistics and became the first woman member of the Royal Statistical Society. Dr John Snow famously used meticulous record-keeping to establish that cholera, the great scourge of Victorian London, was transmitted by infected water, not foul air. And Charles Babbage, generally remembered for his unsuccessful attempts to build a mechanical computer, is also credited with devising the pre-printed survey form. In the twentieth century, the Second World War highlighted the need for reliable statistics to enable the country's leadership to make key decisions.

Thus, as this book points out, Winston Churchill, complaining that 'the utmost confusion is caused when people argue on different statistical data,' ordered the establishment of the Central Statistical Office, one of the predecessor organisations of today's ONS, to consolidate the efforts of other departments and issue 'final authoritative working statistics'. And we've continued that tradition during the pandemic, with, for example, our Coronavirus Infection Study, which measures the actual prevalence of infection, through testing people in a random sample of households across the country, not simply counting the number of positive tests registered on a particular day – something more important than ever in the light of the very rapid spread of the Omicron variant at the beginning of 2022. As I said in the foreword to the first edition of this book, what has happened since the onset of the pandemic is something more or less unprecedented in living memory – there has been nothing like this and on this scale since the Spanish flu outbreak over a hundred years ago. Indeed, one of the recurring themes of this book is the dramatic effect that both the earlier pandemic and also the two vast wars of the twentieth century had on the demography of this country.

In the previous foreword I also looked forward to the fieldwork for the 2021 census in England and Wales, which was pioneering in that it was designed to be digital-first. Soon after this paperback edition comes out, we will be beginning the huge process of publishing the results – but for now I can say that online completion was a great success – 89 per cent of households in England and Wales filled in their forms online (well exceeding our target of 75 per cent), with, overall, 97 per cent of households having responded either digitally or on paper (in case you're interested to know, of those who responded online, 56 per cent used a phone, 35 per cent a desktop computer and 9 per cent a tablet). Moreover, getting on for half those households that were sent paper forms on request actually chose the online option in the end. And there were environmental benefits too – a household responding on paper needed 16 sheets of paper, compared with only one (the letter with an individualised access code) for a household responding electronically. Thus the very high online response rate saved the vast majority of the 450 million sheets of paper that we reckon that a paper-only census would have required.

So please sit back and enjoy Boris Starling's lively take on what official data past and present tell us about our nation, who we are, what we do and where we live. We official statisticians tend not to be a showy bunch, but I hope this new edition will continue to help readers to see from this story why we are quietly passionate about what we do – and why, above all, it matters so much.

INTRODUCTION

In 2011, the year of the previous census for England and Wales, the film *One Day* was released. Based on a bestselling novel by David Nicholls, it told the story of its two protagonists, Emma and Dexter, through the neat structural conceit of visiting them on the same day every year for two decades. As such, the viewer saw Emma and Dexter's lives through snapshots taken at regular intervals, with the changes in those lives signified at least partially through the regular markers humans use: where they were living, what they were doing, the status of their relationships, and so on.

In other words, through a very small-scale and annual census.

This desire – to know, to mark, to record – is one that has existed for millennia. As mankind began to arrange itself into societies of increasing numbers and complexity, so too did the rulers of those societies seek to find ways of enumerating at least what they considered the most important elements of the body politic. Ancient Egypt introduced censuses towards the end of its Middle Kingdom era, roughly 1,800 years before the birth of Christ. The Sumerians and Babylonians also had some form of citizen registration. In the Bible, the Book of Numbers is named after the counting of the Israelite population, and opens with the Lord speaking 'unto Moses in the wilderness of Sinai, in the tabernacle of the congregation, on the first day of the second month, in the second year after they were come out of the land of Egypt, saying, Take ye the sum of all the congregation of the children of Israel, after their families, by the house of their fathers, with the number of their names'. Later, King David ordered Joab, the captain of his host, to count the tribes of Israel and Judah, which came to 800,000 and 500,000 men respectively. For this apparently sinful activity, God sent a pestilence that killed 70,000 men, and the fear of further divine retribution was one of the arguments used in eighteenth-century Britain against enumerating the population. The Chinese began to compile local population registers from the sixth century BC, and the Indians from around the third century BC.

But it was the Romans who first solidified the census into something approximating what we recognise today, and in doing so gave us its name too (from the Latin *censere*, 'to assess'.) The first Roman census was carried out under the orders of Servius Tullius in the sixth century BC, and gradually became an event held every five years and aimed above all at establishing two things: the availability of men of fighting age and the determination of taxes. The most famous census of all was, of course, the one organised in Judaea by Publius Sulpicius Quirinius, the Roman governor of Syria, which became famous not so much for anything that it counted but for the movement of one particular couple. As the Gospel of Luke recounts, and as everyone who goes to a carol service hears during the lessons, 'it came to pass in those days, that there went out a decree from Caesar Augustus that all the world should be taxed. And all went to be taxed, every one into his own city. And Joseph also went up from Galilee, out of the city of Nazareth, into Judaea, unto the city of David, which is called Bethlehem; (because he was of the house and lineage of David:) To be taxed with Mary his espoused wife, being great with child.'

Given that censuses concern themselves first and foremost with hard, quantifiable facts, it is ironic that

Luke's linking the birth of Christ to Quirinius' census is almost certainly wrong on several grounds. Matthew says that the birth of Jesus took place in the reign of Herod, but Herod had died around a decade before the census Luke mentions; no Roman census required people to travel to the distant homes of their ancestors, thus making Joseph and Mary's trip from Galilee to Nazareth extremely unlikely; and the Romans did not at the time impose direct taxation on their client kingdoms. But, as the man who shot Liberty Valance knew, when the legend becomes fact, then print the legend: and so the birth of Christ is always associated with a census.

The first formal English census is only slightly less momentous, coming as it did at the instigation of William the Conqueror and being enshrined in the Domesday Book of 1086. William, perhaps understandably for a man who had basically performed a hostile takeover of an entire country, wanted to know much the same things previous census-takers all over the world had sought: who lived where, who owned what, who had owned it before the Conquest, who could fight and who owed how much in taxes. The *Anglo-Saxon Chronicle* (a collection of historical documents rather than a regional newspaper, which would have been a very early casualty of the digital journalism revolution) reports that William sent 'his men over all England into each shire; commissioning them to find out how many hundreds of hides* were in the shire, what land the king himself had, and what stock upon the land; or, what dues he ought to have by the year from the shire'.

In a move of which modern-day dictators would be proud, the Domesday Book was not only official but unalterable: there was no right of dispute for anyone who felt the assessors had incorrectly calculated their holdings and liabilities. These overtones gave the book the name by which it's known now. Richard FitzNeal, treasurer of England under Henry II, wrote that

> the book is metaphorically called by the native
> English, Domesday, i.e., the Day of Judgement. For
> as the sentence of that strict and terrible last account
> cannot be evaded by any skilful subterfuge, so when
> this book is appealed to on those matters which it
> contains, its sentence cannot be quashed or set aside
> with impunity. That is why we have called the book

---

* A 'hide' was an Anglo-Saxon unit of land measurement, originally reckoned as enough land to support one family.

'the Book of Judgement' ... *not because it contains decisions on various difficult points, but because its decisions, like those of the Last Judgement, are unalterable.*

The book is divided into two parts, Little Domesday (covering Norfolk, Suffolk and Essex) and Great Domesday (pretty much the rest of England at the time, with a few exceptions). Rumours that Little Domesday was so short due to the restricted gene pool of its East Anglian denizens are scurrilous and without foundation, at least according to a resident of Cromer whose brother may also be his wife. Rumours that Great Domesday was written almost entirely by a single scribe are much more credible (and presumably the scribe in question was the first Englishman ever known to have suffered from repetitive strain injury, carpal tunnel syndrome and bouts of incandescent fury when someone pointed out a typo on page 343 of a particularly beautifully illuminated manuscript section). And it was thorough: to take one example almost at random, the small village of Ightfield in Shropshire, or 'Istrefeld' as Domesday calls it, is summed up thus:

Gerard holds Istrefeld. Ulniet held it and was a free man. There two hides pay geld. There is land for four ploughs. A priest is there and two bordars [according to the Oxford English Dictionary, *'a villein of the lowest rank, who held a cottage at his lord's pleasure'], with one plough. Woodland there for fattening sixty swine, and two hayes [a 'haye' being an enclosure constructed for the capture of game, especially roebuck].*

Some efforts were made to gauge the population: for example, in Elizabeth I's reign, the bishops were asked to count the number of families in their respective dioceses and report back to the Privy Council. Later, mid-eighteenth-century proposals to count the population were fiercely attacked in the Commons, either as an affront to traditional British liberties or as a security risk if it meant disclosing our potential weakness to a foreign power (not to mention the risk of another pestilence from God). Indeed, despite the country's increasing prosperity, some people thought the population might actually be falling: for example, in 1780, the Welsh Nonconformist minister the Reverend Richard Price published a book on the subject. Known in short as *Dr Price's Reversionary Payments*, its title runs in full to 60 words, of which the last nine are '*and a Postscript on the Population of the Kingdom*'. In this he argued that the population might have fallen by as much as a quarter in the previous 70 years. Price was, incidentally, a friend of the pioneering statistician Thomas Bayes, the proponent of Bayes's theorem, and was apparently responsible for getting the theorem published after Bayes's death. However, it would be almost three-quarters of a millennium since Domesday before the country finally essayed another formal, general census. Blame it on political opposition, on expense, on successive governments having different priorities, on the country being at war as often as not, but it was not until 1796 that a statistician and former House of Commons clerk named John Rickman (once described as 'hugely literate, oppressively full of infor- mation … from matter of fact to Xenophon and Plato') proposed a census in the *Commercial, Agricultural, and Manufacturer's Magazine* (which sounds very much like one of *Have I Got News for You*'s guest publications, alongside the likes of *Hot Dip Galvanising* or *Cigar Aficionado*). That Rickman also edited the *Commercial, Agricultural, and Manufacturer's Magazine* may suggest that he wasn't the most enormous fun at parties, but on this issue at least he was certainly persuasive. He enumerated 12 reasons as to why a census was necessary, among them the usual questions of taxation and conscription but also the contentions that 'the intimate knowledge of any country must form the rational basis of legislation and diplomacy', that 'an industrious population is the basic power and resource of any nation, and therefore its size needs to be known', that 'the need to plan the production of corn and thus to know the number of people who had to be fed' and that 'the life insurance industry would be stimulated by the results' (there is a certain Alan Partridge quality to the last of these, which may endear him to the modern-day reader). This all tapped very much into Thomas Malthus's concerns of the time about overpopulation (which ran directly opposite to Dr Price's fears), published in his 1798 *Essay on the Principle of Population*.

Thus Rickman's idea took hold, and the necessary legislation, proposed by Mr Abbot, MP for Helston in Cornwall, was rapidly passed by Parliament in late 1800. The first UK census therefore took place on 10 March 1801, and consisted of six questions aimed at working out the national population, their living arrangements and occupations, and giving some idea as to whether the population was increasing or decreasing.

Without an overarching national body to take charge, enumeration in each area was the responsibility of the local overseers of the poor or, failing them, substantial householders and church officials and, if need be, 'constables, tithingmen, headboroughs or other peace officers'.* (In Scotland, early censuses were, by contrast, carried out by local schoolmasters – perhaps a mark of the high esteem that Scotland has traditionally placed on education – but in 1861 responsibility passed to the recently created General Register Office for Scotland, now the National Register of Scotland.) Since there was obviously no previous census against which the last point could be measured, baptism and burial records were requested from each of the previous 20 years and then for the start of each decade before that, all the way back to 1700. The population of England and Wales was found to be 8.9 million, and that of Scotland 1.6 million – almost exactly the same numbers who live in modern-day Greater London and the Glasgow metropolitan area respectively. Ightfield in Shropshire, which in 1086 had had four ploughs, two bordars, a priest and woodland for 60 swine, now boasted a

* These were the traditional officials that parishes appointed to see to law and order.

population of 209 people (which would have risen only to 529 by 2011).

The next census took place in 1811, showing a population of 12 million, an increase of 15 per cent over the decade. With one exception – that of 1941, which was cancelled due to the small matter of the Second World War being in full swing, though even that was partially offset by the drawing up of a wartime National Register at the start of the war in 1939 – so it has stayed to the present day: a census every year ending with a '1'. (Tottenham Hotspur fans of a certain age will remember when those years were reliable sources of glory: the League in 1951, the League and FA Cup double in 1961, the Cup in 1981 and 1991. Spurs fans of younger vintage, used to altogether sparser pickings in the silverware department, will regard years ending in '1' rather like all other years, as for them all years end in zero.)

The census has not, of course, stayed still. Categories have been added, changed and removed; questions asked and suspended. In 1821, respondents' ages were included for the first time, albeit in quinquennial groups (categories nowadays familiar to marathon runners and triathletes whose advancing years are brutally marked out in black and white: MV45 for men's veterans 45–49, FV50 for female veterans 50–54, and so on). 1821 saw the first census in Ireland, which was of course then in its entirety part of the UK. The early enumerators there were mostly appointed from local tax collectors, apparently on the theory that, like the Poor Law officials in England and Wales, they would be familiar with their districts.

The 1841 census saw a seismic shift in the way the count was organised and conducted. Whereas the three previous censuses had been fundamentally myriad local affairs subsequently tallied together, which had left substantial scope for people being counted twice or not at all, responsibility in England and Wales was now passed to the recently created post of registrar general. A trial run was carried out to see how many households an enumerator could cover in a single day – the forerunner of today's census tests and rehearsals. In consequence, 35,000 enumerators were appointed to take the census in the shortest possible time, and all records were to be sent to London for analysis at the General Register Office. In addition, proper information on every member of a household was now sought, and all the data collected were published in three separate volumes: the Enumeration Abstract, the Age Abstract and the Occupation Abstract, which sound like long-lost Robert Ludlum novels. If 1801 was the first modern British census, 1841 was the first one to do things as they are in effect still done today: the principles of enumeration have not really been altered since, although the methods have been updated by such developments as printed forms and the development of next year's primarily online census. Ironically, Rickman himself did not quite live to see the introduction of what might be termed census version 2.0: he had died the previous year.

The census continued to become more advanced and complex as it entered its second half-century and beyond. 1851 asked for exact ages rather than quinquennial age-groups, marriage status, and also noted blindness, deafness and dumbness. It also asked about religion – interestingly, as a voluntary question, as it was when it reappeared on the form in 2001. It asked about attendance at services, rather than affiliation, and was aimed primarily at establishing whether there was sufficient provision of churches and other places of worship. The subsequent report opined that, 'The most important fact which this investigation as to attendance brings before us is, unquestionably, the alarming number of the non-attendants'. It was clear who was responsible for this; not of course the middle and upper classes, but 'artizans' and 'the labouring classes'. 1871 asked for those who were classified as a lunatic, or as an idiot or imbecile. On one level, this seems amusing to us – we all know people of whom we would say, hopefully teasingly, that they fall into at least one of these categories, and in some cases all three – but it is also a salutary reminder that Victorian attitudes towards the mentally infirm now seem at best unenlightened and at worst actively cruel. The term 'idiot' survived until 1901, when it was replaced with 'feeble-minded'.

In 1881, a new dictionary of occupations was drawn up to keep pace with rapid changes in industry and the proliferation of new jobs. Around 12,000 different occupations were listed, almost double the previous amount, though by 1911 this would be up to around 30,000 (much same as in the coding index of the latest 2020 Standard Occupational Classification, though the latter no longer includes 'wheeltapper' but does acknowledge 'YouTuber' as a recognised occupation). 1881 also saw respondents in Scotland asked whether they spoke Gaelic, a question extended to Welsh-speaking in Wales in 1891. 1901 saw unmarried women differentiated from their married or widowed counterparts for the first time. The 1901 census presciently asked people in certain industries whether they worked from their own homes, though presumably it failed to foresee that in another 120 years the main question for homeworkers would be 'Are you still on mute?' as they tried to conduct yet another online meeting with their widely scattered colleagues. In 1911 – the first census to use machines, albeit by our standards rather primitive ones which worked via holes punched in appropriate positions on special cards – the fertility of marriage was included, with questions asked about the duration of existing marriages and the number of living children born to each marriage. However, the outbreak of war in 1914 delayed the processing of the fertility data, the last report of which was not published until 1923, a dozen years after its collection.

The 1921 census in Great Britain was held in the aftermath of the First World War and the Spanish flu – see Part Four. But it was postponed in all of Ireland, north and south, because of the political situation. In Northern Ireland it was not held until 1926, carried out by the registrar general for Northern Ireland, and the timetable for Northern Ireland did not get back in sync with the rest of the UK until 1951. The 1931 census went off without a hitch, but 11 years later all the results were destroyed in a fire at an Office of Works store in Hayes, Middlesex. It also saw clerks downgraded to Social Class III, having been already moved down from Social Class I to Social Class II two decades earlier – this gradual fall seemingly a result of the spread of universal education (and typewriters) devaluing skills that had once been in great demand. 1951 introduced a 1 per cent sample to allow a quick and wide cross-section of data before the actual publication of the full results, and asked each household about their water supply as these began to shift away from communal arrangements and outdoor toilets to individual and internal household ones. A piped internal supply was deemed different from a tap in the yard, and a tap in the yard of course different from a public standpipe: a water closet was distinct from an earth or chemical one. In 1961, an electronic computer – an IBM 705, to be precise – was used to help process results for the first time, and like all computers of the era took up most of a room and yet had less processing power than the SIM card in the smartphone on which you may well be reading this. As the General Register Office did not yet have its own computer, one located in Winchester belonging to the Royal Army Pay Corps was used instead. The 1971 census was the first to be conducted under the aegis of the Office of Population Censuses and Surveys, which had been set up the previous year to combine the General Register Office and the Government Social Survey. And questions on ethnicity and religion were introduced (or reintroduced) in 1991 and 2001 respectively. In 2001 responsibility for the census passed to the Office for National Statistics, which had come into being five years earlier when the Office of Population Censuses and Surveys merged with the Central Statistical Office. And 2021 saw for the first time census fieldwork carried out in England, Wales and Northern Ireland on a 'digital-first' completion basis.

The census has been compulsory since 1921, but at least two years' censuses have been subject to boycotts by way of civil disobedience. In 1911, the Women's Freedom League encouraged women to avoid the census (by attending all-night parties or staying with friends) as part of the suffragette movement campaigning for women's right to vote. Emily Davison, who two years later would die after colliding with by the king's horse at the Derby, was recorded in two places on census night: her own house in Russell Square and a broom cupboard in the Houses of Parliament. And opposition to Margaret Thatcher's poll tax (not to mention fear that the census might be used to enforce that tax) led to press reports that up to a million people had avoided the 1991 census, even though Mrs Thatcher herself had stepped down as prime minister the previous year and the poll tax was clearly on the way out.

Of course, for the more recent censuses, one can't yet see the actual records themselves, only the anonymised data tables that are published. This is because these records, full as they are of very sensitive personal information, remain confidential for a hundred years after they are collected, so that the 1921 census returns have only just been published. Once that period has elapsed, census returns are in the public domain, and these days can be easily accessed online, thanks to popular genealogy websites. But until then they remain closely guarded by the ONS. Not so long ago the well-known television crime drama *Silent Witness* featured the cops logging in to an imaginary 'National Census Database' to get the information they needed to crack the case; but, alas, thanks to the hundred-year rule, it would have to be a pretty cold case review indeed for the police to be able to access any useful information from the census (anyone fancy digging around the 1891 census returns to propose yet another suspect for being

Jack the Ripper?). Indeed, data confidentiality generally, and the need to avoid accidentally releasing material that could identify individuals, is very important to the ONS, which means that it can't always release information in the full level of detail that it collects. For example, on baby names, it doesn't publish those names that are only given to one or two individual babies each year.

Meanwhile, quite distinct from the decennial census, more and more official statistics were being collected, often reflecting particular concerns. For example, the registration of births, marriages and deaths had long been done by the Church of England on a parish-by-parish basis, but with the spread of other denominations that could not carry out legally binding weddings according to their own law, there was increasing pressure for a registration system controlled by the state not the church. This resulted in the Registration Act and the Marriage Act 1836, under which Thomas Lister was appointed the first registrar general for England and Wales. And naturally with the registers came the statistical reports: Lister's first annual report, published in 1839, revealed that, in the 12-month period of July 1837 to June 1838, there were 107,201 marriages celebrated 'according to the

Rites of the Established Church' and another 111,481 not according to those rites. Again, the late nineteenth and early twentieth centuries were times of labour unrest, not least the 1888 match girls' strike and the 1889 London dockers' strike. Not surprisingly, therefore, the official statistics on labour disputes, first compiled by the Board of Trade and then the Department of Employment but more recently by the Office for National Statistics, went back to 1891 – though the peak year for the number of days lost to strikes did not come until 1926, with the General Strike and the long-running miners' strike that followed it.

Incidentally, different arrangements were already starting to apply to the different countries of the United Kingdom, even in those pre-devolution days: thus, while England and Wales had a registrar general from 1836, the first registrar general for Scotland was not appointed until 1854 and civil registration in Ireland only began in 1864. To this day, the ONS is responsible for the census only in England and Wales, with National Records for Scotland (set up in 2011) and the Northern Ireland Statistics and Research Agency (established in 1996) now looking after it elsewhere in the UK. This means that sometimes, especially when dealing with old series going a long way back, it can be hard to get long-run numbers for the UK as a whole.

Quite separately, the great advances in computing in recent decades have made possible a number of developments in the collection and analysis of official data. For example, in late 2019 the ONS began publishing, jointly with HM Revenue and Customs, monthly updates on the number of employees on the payroll in the UK. A few months later, when the country was struck by the coronavirus pandemic, forcing many businesses to suspend trading, the ONS was able to accelerate its timetable for publishing these figures so as to get them out quicker than was possible with the old survey-based measures of employment. Since then the range of information released from this dataset has been greatly widened. Likewise, as part of its work to meet the challenge of providing richer and more real-time statistics to inform decision-makers, in 2016 the ONS announced the establishment of a data science campus. This was seen as a way of exploring and using innovative methods and new data sources, including administrative data and big data, to improve existing statistics and develop new outputs for the public good.

The campus continues to play an important role in the data revolution by innovating public sector data science and building artificial intelligence (AI) capability through a range of learning and development programmes, in collaboration with other government departments, industry and academia. Since its launch in 2017, it has researched a large number of different topics – including investigating the use of machine-learning techniques to predict missing energy performance scores in the housing stock; the use of open data sets to develop a better understanding of loneliness; using non-traditional data sources to understand the characteristics of high-growth companies; and using tax returns, ship-tracking data and road traffic sensor data to allow early identification of large economic changes. Moreover, it too was able to respond rapidly to the pandemic; for example, doing analysis of anonymised mobility data released by Google to give insight into the impact of social distancing measures introduced in response to the pandemic.

This book uses the census snapshots over the past two centuries, as well as other figures from the Office for National Statistics and other official sources, to chart the past and present of this country during that period; to see, as far as possible, how much we have changed, and indeed how much we have stayed the same. It is not, and does not aim to be, an overarching or definitive history of the country – such a thing would run to the length of the *Encyclopaedia Britannica* – but rather a broad and hopefully light-hearted look at what the censuses, surveys and other official statistics have thrown up.

It is divided into three main sections: who we are, what we do and where we live.

'Who we are' looks at, among other things, how family arrangements have changed, how we spend our free time, our religious and cultural beliefs, and what the state of education can tell us about what young people do and don't want to do with their lives.

'What we do' examines how our working lives have evolved over those two centuries, a period which has spanned not just an Industrial Revolution but a technological one too. It looks, among other things, at the jobs that exist now but did not in the past, and vice versa; at the effects of automation; and at the extent to which gender roles in work have changed.

'Where we live' covers not only changes in local areas but also the wider country too, and in particular the shift to predominantly urban ways of living, and also how housing tenure has altered. This is a small and crowded island, and yet there are still substantial swathes that are, to all intents and purposes, scarcely inhabited, as our look at population density shows.

These are followed by two shorter sections – 'A Census of Enlightenment', looking back a hundred years to the 1921 census, held in the aftermath of the First World War and the devastating Spanish flu pandemic, and 'Back to the Future?', where I look forward a hundred years and speculate a little about what a 2121 census might look like.

Of course, there are limits to what is, or ought to be, collected in official statistics, which are after all funded out of the taxes we all have to pay to the government. Thus, among the questions that have stumped the normally indefatigable ONS press office down the years were: 'How many rats and squirrels are there in the UK?', 'What's the number of people in the UK who sing in a choir?', 'What percentage of the UK are aristocrats?', 'How many ovens break down on Christmas Day?' and even 'Do you have statistics on how many new statistics start getting collected or published every year?' But while we don't really *need* to know how many people sing in a choir, things like the number of people who are born every year, how many get married, how many are in work or what we are dying of, are things that the country and its decision-makers really do need to know.

This book was great fun and rather illuminating to write, and I hope you feel the same way about reading it. If you do, and you're approached by the ONS at some point in the future to take part in one of its surveys, please bear in mind that, without people like you helping, much of the information here just couldn't have been compiled.

PART ONE

WHO WE ARE

At the most basic level, the census is a once-a-decade snapshot of who we are: how we're born, how we live and how we die. This section deals with all three of those, and in that order (it's a fairly obvious order, after all). It looks at fertility rates and maternal ages, at family structures and living patterns, and at death rates and causes. All these are revealing in any number of ways, but behind the figures, no less present for being unseen and no less real for being unquantifiable, are the characteristics of the nation and those who live here.

Who are we? We like to see ourselves as amusing, decent, fair, polite and tolerant. We root for the underdog and like to take people down a peg or two when they've become too big for their boots. We like laws and rules, especially unwritten ones: at the battle of Trafalgar, for example, Admiral Cuthbert Collingwood refused to place snipers in the rigging because that wasn't the way proper chaps won naval battles. We're an island race, and it shows in our psyche. We regard our homes as our castles and consider ourselves self-contained and self-sufficient. We don't go in for overt displays of patriotism – no saluting the flag, no pledges of allegiance – but give us a special occasion, such as a royal jubilee, and you could circle the earth with the amount of Union Jack bunting that comes out. Even in an age where deference has largely gone and globalisation is ever more prevalent, we continue to define ourselves by class and region. We apologise at the drop of a hat: for things we've done, for things we haven't done, for things we might yet do and things we might yet not do, for being late, being early and being on time. We would rather shrivel up and die than make a scene.* We like our upper lips to be stiff and our calm to be kept while carrying on. We like queuing and listening to a shipping forecast for areas we will never visit.

---

* This horror at having our reserve eroded extends to public transport. In 2016 a well-meaning but misguided man made up some 'Tube chat' badges for people on the London Underground to wear if they welcomed conversation from strangers. Londoners were horrified at this peculiar kind of fresh hell. Resentful silence while staring furiously at their phones is the preferred London way of Tube travel. As far as Londoners were concerned, only three types of people spoke on the Tube: drunks, lunatics and Americans. (The man behind the #tubechat initiative was, perhaps inevitably, from Colorado.)

There are many things you could put into a 'what it means to be British' list, but surely one of the most British things of all is the horror of even thinking about making such a list. In that regard, perhaps, the census is rather un-British, comprising as it does of all sorts of lists; but then again maybe the only thing more British than the horror of making a list of what it means to be British is to find the entire nation numerated and tabulated by a plethora of lists.

BIRTH

'THIS IS WHERE WE CAME IN ...'

Live births in the UK were consistently above 1 million in the years up to the First World War. Thereafter there have been only four years with births above a million – 1920, 1921, 1947 and 1964. The first three were all rebounds from low wartime levels; the last was the tail end of the post-war 'baby boom' (a concept now repurposed as a mark of youthful derision with the dismissive 'OK, Boomer'), which itself really began in 1947, thus neatly bookending the boom with two record years.

It should come as little surprise that the average age of parents is on the rise, not just for first children but for all live births. Figure 2 goes back to just before the Second World War for mothers and to 1964 for fathers (conveniently within the timeframe as laid out by Philip Larkin in a famous quotation on the start of sexual intercourse).

Fathers are consistently around three years older than mothers (another thing that may come as little surprise to anyone who's seen how girls mature quicker than boys during adolescence, a process which often seems to stall for boys well into adulthood). The trend in the age of mothers was clearly downwards in the early part of this period, though with a blip relating to the later years of the Second World War (when, as in

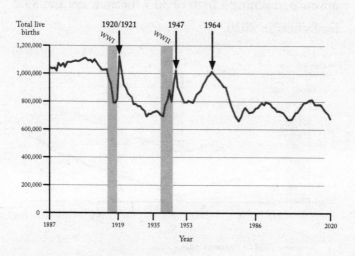

Figure 1: Total UK births
Source: Office for National Statistics

the First World War, there were fewer young men around and therefore less opportunity for marriage and procreation).

The mid-seventies saw the average age for both parents at its lowest (1973–5 represented the trough for mothers at 26.4 years, and 1974 for fathers at 29.4), which if nothing else proves that the various heinous crimes against fashion inflicted by clothes designers of the era had little effect on the libido of those obliged to wear such monstrosities of flared brown velour. Since then the trend has been pretty consistently upwards, reaching a high of 30.7 for mothers and 33.7 for fathers in 2020.

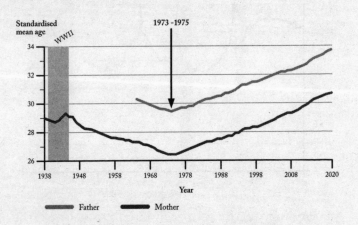

Figure 2: Average age of parents in England and Wales
Source: Office for National Statistics

For biological, financial and social reasons, the vast majority of births are to mothers between the ages of 20 and 40, but of course there is always a small proportion of those who fall outside those parameters. In 1938, the last year before the disruption caused by the Second World War, the over-40s accounted for more births than the under-20s, which may be a slight surprise given that some women married more or less straight out of school in those days and that fertility treatment was not yet available. A decade or so later, younger mothers were indeed accounting for a higher proportion of births than their older counterparts, a pattern which became more prevalent over the years. By 1972 mothers under 20 comprised 11 per cent of the total, and by 1982 those over 40 only 1 per cent, but since then the gap between the two has closed again. Indeed, in 2013 both groups accounted for exactly the same proportion of births, at 4.2 per cent.

If we divide the 20–40 age range into quartiles, the 25–29 and 30–34 cohorts together account for 60 per cent of births, with 20–24 and 35–39 coming in at 40 per cent combined. And within these two highest-performing quartiles (this is rapidly taking on the shape of *Who Wants to Be a Millionaire?*, with the computer taking away two random wrong answers), the preponderance of each has waxed and waned as average birth ages for mothers have first decreased and then increased again. Team 25–29 held the advantage in the post-war years, but by the 1970s the two lines were converging, and now Team 30–34 are in the ascendancy.

The decline in fertility rates is not confined to the UK, of course. The vast majority of Western Europe is experiencing a similar phenomenon, with profound long-term social implications. Below an average 'total fertility rate'* of about 2.1 children per woman, the population would eventually begin to shrink (provided mortality rates remain constant and net migration has no effect). This so-called 'replacement rate' is the level of fertility at which a population exactly replaces itself from one generation to the next. In developed countries, where child mortality is low, replacement level fertility requires an average of roughly 2.1 children per woman. In countries with high infant and child mortality rates, however, the average number of births

---

* The total fertility rate is defined in full as 'the average number of live children that a group of women would each bear if they experienced the age-specific fertility rates of the calendar year in question throughout their childbearing lifespan'. This figure stood at 1.59 for England in 2020, down from 1.71 in 2018.

may need to be much higher. This number is higher than 2 because even in developed countries not all children survive to adulthood and because, on average, 105 boys are born for every 100 girls (the figure is of course higher for countries with higher rates of infant mortality).

A study published in *The Lancet* followed world trends in fertility rates from 1950 to 2017. The global average at the start of the period in question was 4.7; by the end it was 2.4. But larger family sizes in the developing world (4.6 in sub-Saharan Africa, 2.7 in North Africa and the Middle East) mask the fact that, like the UK, many developed countries now have a birth rate of less than two.

The average completed family size for women who reached the age of 45 in 2020 (having been born in 1975) was 1.92 children per woman, fractionally more than for those women born a few years earlier but lower than in the past – records, which begin in 1920, peaked at 2.42 for women born in 1934 and 1935. These latter would, of course, have been having their offspring during the 'baby boom' years. Further comparisons between the generations are also instructive. The average age of mothers at childbirth (for all children, not merely the first) has gone from 29.0 in

1938 down to a low of 26.4 in mid-70s and back up to 30.7 in 2020. In all, 67 per cent of the 1920-born cohort were mothers by the age of 30, a figure that had dropped to 52 per cent for women born in 1975. Of the class of 1975, two-children families remained the most common family size (37 per cent), with 17 per cent having a single child and 18 per cent remaining childless. The proportion of one-time mothers has dropped only slightly over the years (21 per cent of women born in 1920 had only one child), but that of childless women fell from 21 per cent for the 1920 cohort to 9 per cent for the 1946 cohort before rising once more to its current level.

The latter has several possible causes. Fewer women are getting married than before; some women prefer to remain childless in order to focus on their careers; others postpone decisions on whether to have children until it's biologically too late either way; and the more women who remain childless through choice or otherwise, the more acceptable and uncontroversial that lifestyle becomes. There is also considerable evidence that having children does not actually make people any happier, indeed quite the opposite: a 22-country study published in the *American Journal of Sociology* in 2016 found a considerable 'parenting happiness gap', with non-parents significantly happier than parents. (It's not known whether the methodology included posing the questions at 3 a.m. on a Saturday night, when non-parents would be out clubbing and parents were trying to get a fractious infant back to sleep.)

Why are fertility rates falling? There is much media attention on factors such as declining sperm counts, but while average sperm count has indeed dropped (by more than 50 per cent in the West between 1970 and 2011, from 99 million sperm per millilitre of semen to 47 million, according to the 2017 *Human Reproduction Update*), it is still well within normal reproductive range (anything above 15 million). Aside from the obvious effects of medical advances on child mortality, thus obviating the perceived need for larger families to compensate for some children failing to make it to adulthood, the fall in fertility rates is therefore more social than physiological. Women have greater access to contraception than their ancestors, plus more varied and challenging education and career opportunities, which allow them to delay childbirth till later. In addition, the rising costs of living extend to child raising (the ONS 2019–20 *Family Spending* report found that households with two adults and two children spent on average £801 a week, compared with

£665 for households with just two adults), and many couples would prefer not overly to compromise their lifestyle standards by having more children than they feel they could reasonably afford. And some couples regard not having children as morally the right thing to do, particularly in environmental terms.

While there are plenty of social and economic reasons for women to have children later in life, in purely biological terms it still makes sense not to delay childbearing: society moves much quicker than biology does. Younger women are more likely to become pregnant and less likely to suffer miscarriages. Natural fertility peaks in the early 20s, gradually declines from around 25 to 35, and then begins to decline much more rapidly after the age of 35.

Lower fertility rates, combined with increased life expectancy, eventually lead to an ageing population, with the attendant strains on individuals and society: later retirements, greater reliance on healthcare, lesser numbers of young people coming into the employment market, and so on. To a degree this can be mitigated by factors such as immigration and artificial intelligence, though neither of these are without issues.

Just as birth rates are declining, so too are conception rates: they dropped in seven out of the nine years

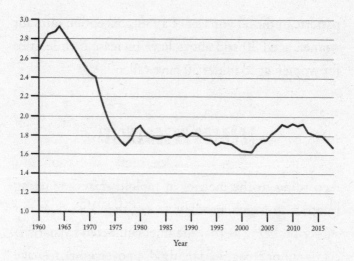

Figure 3: Global fertility rate
Source: Institute for Health Metrics and Evaluation at the
University of Washington

from 2011 to 2019, in fact. Conception rates, unlike birth rates, are by necessity subject to estimation. In 2019, there were an estimated 821,089 conceptions to women of all ages in England and Wales, a decrease of 2.1 per cent on the previous year, though for a fourth year running, women aged 40 and over saw an increase in conceptions (and indeed were the only group to do so), with a rate of 16.7 conceptions per 1,000 women aged over 40. This is perhaps the most extreme indicator of the gradual age increase in mothers, a 30–30–30 pattern: in the 30 years since 1990, conception rates for women aged 30 and above have increased while rates for women aged under 30 have fallen.

TEENAGE PREGNANCIES

According to the metrics of tabloid scaremongering (metrics to which, needless to say, the ONS does not subscribe, being as they are unencumbered by statistical rigour or recognised methods of oversight), teenage pregnancies were some years ago right up there with uncontrolled immigration, forecasts of extreme weather, NHS tourism, benefit fraud and the EU. Certain media outlets would have had you believe that pretty much every teenage girl in the land was a feckless sex maniac getting herself knocked up by an equally feckless boy and condemning mother and child to a life on benefits.

This image became so prevalent that it skews public attitudes on the issue. For example, what percentage of girls aged under 16 do you think became pregnant in 2014? If you guessed 10, you were on the low side, and if 20, you were on the high side – but, crucially, those sides are of the average guess rather than the reality.

The average guess is 15 per cent; the actual figure is 0.5 per cent. That is, of every 200 girls under 16, only one becomes pregnant; and the average person overestimates this by a factor of 30.

These figures haven't always been so low, and that they've come down in the past couple of decades is no accident (unlike many of the very pregnancies in question). In 1999, cognisant that teenage pregnancy rates were running ahead of much of the rest of Europe, the government launched a 10-year Teenage Pregnancy Strategy. Together with encouraging young women to gain greater educational qualifications, this strategy included improved guidance on sex and relationships, improved access to contraception and sexual health services, and information about the higher risk of infant mortality in very young mothers. Alison Hadley, who was in charge of the strategy, said: 'We realised that teenage pregnancy was everyone's business, from health to education, to social care and youth services.'

A gradual initial decline has accelerated slightly since the financial crisis of 2008, and now conception rates for women aged under 18 have decreased by almost two-thirds since 1999. The 2019 figure of 15.8 conceptions per 1,000 women aged 15 to 17 years is the lowest since records began.

WHAT DID YOU JUST CALL ME?

Few statistics capture the public's imagination like baby names. What people call their children, and why, is a source of perennial fascination; names coming into and going out of fashion, the influence of celebrities and so on. Every year the ONS publishes its list of popular names for new arrivals in England and Wales, and to judge by the number of clicks it gets on the website, this is the most popular statistics they produce. One can only speculate what this says about the public appetite for statistics, but how what we're calling the next generation changes year by year is clearly something we can all relate to.

All baby names are recorded on birth registration forms and the ONS tabulates them for England and Wales. Those names that occur at least three times are published; those where only one or two babies were given the name in question are not published, for reasons of confidentiality. Statistics are based on the exact spelling of the name given on the birth certificate; grouping names with similar pronunciation would change the rankings. This causes a great deal of debate – for example, Muhammad was the fifth most popular name for boys in 2020, though if variant spellings were added in then it would of course be higher. However, the same could also be said about plenty of other names – Ann and Anne; Catherine, Katherine and Kathryn; Ian and Iain (which, anyway, are both arguably the same as 'John', of which they are the Celtic equivalents); and so on. Therefore the only practicable position is for the ONS to treat all variant spellings as names in their own right.

Half a century or so seems the maximum for names to retain high levels of popularity. Looking at years that end in a '4' (to make a change from censuses in years ending in '1'), only two names, one male and one female, have remained in the top 10 for six consecutive decades. John was top of the pops in 1914, 1924, 1934 and 1944, second in 1954 and fifth in 1964. Margaret was seventh in 1904, second in 1914, topped the charts for the next three decades and was fourth in 1954. Since then they have both fallen away, and neither made their respective top 100 in 2014.

Whether they will one day begin to recover remains to be seen, but there is evidence that some names do bounce back over the course of many decades. George, for example, was third in 1904, 1914 and 1924, then gradually fell away and bottomed out at 83rd in 1974, but has since climbed back to as high as seventh in 2014. Thomas was also in the top 10 for the first part of the century, and though its fall was never as precipitous as George's (never lower than 40th), it has been consistently higher since then too: top in 1994, third in 2004 and sixth in 2014.

The same holds true, albeit at lower levels, for flower names: Violet, Rose, Daisy, Lily and Poppy. The first four were all in the top 50 in 1904, but gradually fell away over the following decades; by 1944 none of them were in the top 100, and they stayed that way until at least 1994. At the last count in 2014, Violet was 71st, Rose 62nd, Daisy 24th, Lily ninth and Poppy – which had never featured in the top 100 before the twenty-first century – fifth. The most popular toponym (that is, a name borrowed from a place) has historically been Florence: second in 1904 (at least partly because of Florence Nightingale, who at the time was one of the best-known women in the country and indeed had been so for many decades), it fell out of the top 100 in 1944 but returned to rank 26th in 2014. Florence's sister Tuscan city, Siena, was perhaps the ultimate source for the name Sienna, which was seven places higher at 19th.

Certain trends seem easy to identify, at least in part, and especially when it comes to royalty. Take William, for example. It was top for boys in 1904, second in 1914 and 1924, and third in 1934, then dropped to ninth in 1944, 15th in 1954, 29th in 1964, and 41st in 1974. But it climbed to 34th in 1984 and 19th in 1994, and for the past two decades has been in the top 10 (eighth in 2004 and tenth in 2014). It's surely no coincidence that the upward climb coincided with the birth of Prince William in 1982 and his ever-increasing visibility in public life since then. The name of his grandmother, Elizabeth, also received a bump in 1954 (eighth, up from 15th in the previous decade, before it would fall to 20th in 1964) after her coronation the previous year. (However, the same has not held true for Charles, which fell out in the top 10 in 1924, sunk as low as 70th in 1974, and has been no higher than 44th since then.)

There has been far more stability in boys' names than girls' names over the last 100 years. From 1904 through to 2014, 284 unique boys' names have featured in the top 100, compared with 360 girls' names. Of the 14 names that have appeared in every top 100 from 1904 through to 2014, only two are girls (Elizabeth and Sarah); the boys can boast a dozen (Alexander, Charles, Daniel, David, Edward, George, James, Joseph, Michael, Robert, Thomas and William). And when it comes to one-hit wonders – names that have only appeared in one decade's top 100 – the girls outnumber the boys by almost three to one, with 55 against 20 (and, as Figures 4 and 5 show, the disparity has come entirely in more recent decades). In other words, girls' names seem more subject to the whims of fashion than do boys' names.

And, perhaps unsurprisingly, the range of names in use is wider now than it ever has been before. This is almost certainly a cultural shift, in more ways than one: an obvious issue of demographics in an increasingly multicultural society, but also a willingness on the part of parents, irrespective of ethnicity, to choose more unusual, even daring, names. And this is also a relatively recent phenomenon. For boys born in 1996, nearly three-quarters were given a name in that year's top 100; by 2007 this had dropped to three-fifths, and in 2020 it was less than half. Girls' names were less concentrated on the top 100 anyway, but here too the proportion has been falling – from three-fifths having a top 100 name in 1996 to less than half in 2007 and two-fifths in 2020. The proportion of children with names with only one or two instances (that is, too small to be officially published) has also been rising – for boys it went from 4.5 per cent in 1996 to 8.1 per cent

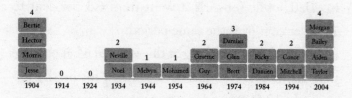

Figure 4: Boys' names that appeared in the top
100 in only one decade
Source: Office for National Statistics

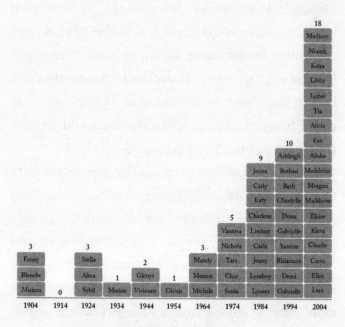

Figure 5: Girls' names that appeared in the top
100 in only one decade
Source: Office for National Statistics

in 2020, while for girls it went from 6.3 per cent to 10.4 per cent over the same period.

Another way of looking at this is to see what proportion of the total number is accounted for by the top name. In 1944, when John was the top boys' name, no fewer than one in 12 male babies were Johns, but thereafter the proportion of boys accounted for by the top name has fallen steadily: in 1964 one in 18 were Davids, in 1984 one in 25 were called Christopher, but by 2014 Oliver could come top of the table despite accounting for just one in 54. For girls, again the popularity of the top name has declined (though not quite in a straight line): in 1944, one in 22 baby girls was called Margaret, but in 2014 Amelia could top the chart with just one in 64 baby girls called that.

The rising popularity of names that would once have been unusual is driven by younger mothers rather than older ones. More 'traditional' names, such as Alexander, Joshua, William, Thomas, Charlotte, Jessica and Sophie, tend to be more popular among older mothers, especially those over 35; but mothers below 25 are more likely to go for names such as Hunter, Logan, Nevaeh and Harper.

The last of these is also a good example of how celebrity culture can influence baby names. In 2011,

Harper was the 858th most popular girls' name; in 2020 it was 28th. It's surely safe to say that this rise has more to do with the birth of Harper Beckham (sister to Brooklyn, Romeo and Cruz) than the death of *To Kill a Mockingbird* author Harper Lee, no matter how much the literati might like to imagine otherwise. These things work both ways, of course: the number of baby girls named Alexa more than halved between 2017 and 2018, following Amazon's introduction of the Alexa electronic voice assistant/virtual encyclopaedia/insufferable know-it-all, and by 2020 the number of new Alexas – babies not smart devices, that is – was barely a twentieth what it had been just three years earlier. (Far be it from this book to offer advice to the richest man in the world, but there must be a niche for a Teenage Alexa device that responds to any question by either slamming a door, turning up the music or tutting dismissively.)

The trend towards variety and informality can also be seen with the growth of names that would once have been seen as informal abbreviations of a proper name (Harry, Charlie, Alfie, Archie, Evie, Millie and so on). This is especially the case for boys: the 2020 top 100 includes 16 names that might be considered diminutives, with 12 of those in the top 50 (up from eight and three respectively in 1994, and five and two in 1904). For girls it's less pronounced: only four diminutives in total in 2020, down from five in 1994.

Baby names are cyclical, and some of them can seem to adhere to a 100-year rule, whereby names popular a century ago can come back into fashion as modern couples reclaim old-fashioned monikers of their grandparents or even great-grandparents. The logic is clear: that enough time has passed for these names to lose their association with the immediately preceding generation (and of course this taps into the kind of retro chic also often seen in fashion and music). So, while names such as Nigel, Derek, Clive, Trevor, Sharon, Lorraine, Anthea and Tracey have largely fallen out of fashion, it's entirely possible that one day they will be seen as mysterious and historical, and will be coming back in for babies born in 2060 or thereabouts. (It's also of course possible that Elon Musk will have started such a craze that every child by then will be called X Æ A-Xii.)

LIFE

HAPPY FAMILIES?

There are probably no metrics to check the truth of Tolstoy's dictum that happy families are alike but unhappy ones are all unhappy in their own way. However, from the data we can say that there are 19.4 million families (by which we mean 'a married, civil partnered or cohabiting couple with or without children, or a lone parent, with at least one child, who live at the same address') in the UK at the last estimate (2020), an increase of 1.4 per cent on the previous year and of 7.4 per cent over the decade from 2010 to 2020. Married or civil partner couples account for two-thirds of families, with cohabiting couples at 18 per cent and lone parents at 15 per cent. There are regional varia-tions, of course, with the 2020 proportion of married families being highest in the South East at 72 per cent and lowest in the North East at 61 per cent.

As we've already seen, the regulation of marriage – which in those days meant opposite-sex couples only, of course – by the state rather than the church was a key driver in the establishment of the registration system in the nineteenth century, and this in turn allowed the registrars to compile the figures. The number of marriages every year gradually rose in line with the growing population until the early 1970s, since when it has been declining. The record peacetime year for weddings was 1972, when there were 480,285 across the UK (though 1939 and 1940, at the start of the Second World War had seen higher numbers, no doubt because of the changing circumstances facing prospective couples as the country mobilised). Since 1972, the number of marriages has been generally declining, to reach 270,286 in 2018 – of which 7,904 were of same-sex couples. Since the introduction of civil weddings their popularity has been growing at the expense of religious ceremonies – in 1842 98.0 per cent of weddings in England and Wales were religious, but by 2018 this had fallen to 21.1 per cent. No doubt this was connected with the introduction of civil weddings at approved venues, often stately homes or country hotels, as opposed to register offices – in 1996, its first full year, this covered just 9.3 per cent of civil weddings in England and Wales; but by 2017, this had risen to 90.4 per cent.

Same-sex married couples are the fastest growing type of same-sex family, having increased by 40 per cent to 212,000 between 2015 and 2019. This is of course due to the 2014 legalisation of same-sex marriage, and though cohabiting couples still remain the most common type of same-sex couple family, the proportion decreased from 59.6 per cent in 2015 to 51.6 per cent in 2019.

Multi-family households (consisting of two or more families) are the fastest growing household type in the country, increasing by two-thirds from 167,000 in 1996 to 279,000 in 2020. The growth in the number of multi-family households could reflect a growth in multi-generational families choosing to live together, or out of necessity because of reasons such as housing affordability, childcare responsibilities and caring for older relatives. However, they still represent the smallest share of households (and of course it's easier to grow rapidly, at least in proportional terms, when you start from a small base). Then again, it worked for *Dallas* back in the day, so don't knock it till you've tried it. (That was a plot hole that was never properly explained: why does one of Texas's premier oil families all live together in one house? Couldn't they afford places of their own?)

Lone-parent families have increased 16.8 per cent since 1996, though interestingly the vast majority of this increase came early on, and over the last 10 years the number has fallen back. Unsurprisingly, lone mothers account for 85 per cent of lone-parent families.

Over the last two decades the number of young people aged 20 to 34 years (so, by definition, counting as 'non-dependent' children) living with their parents has risen by about half, increasing from 2.4 million in 1999 to 3.6 million in 2020. This is equivalent to well over a quarter of young adults of the same age group living with their parents has risen by about half, and may be explained by staying in education and training for longer, formalising relationships and having children at older ages, and increased costs in renting or buying a home. Alternatively, it could be because we are slowly morphing into Italy, where young men live with their mothers well into their 30s before, with great pomp, circumstance, hugging, kissing and general operatic carry-on, they move out and into the flat downstairs.

Family sizes have fluctuated quite severely over the years, with the number of children per marriage at one stage rising to more than double what is today. In 1871 the average family contained 4.3 children; a century later this was down to 2, and now it's round about 1.8.

The reasons for this are varied. Most obviously, perhaps, is the vast improvement in rates of infant mortality: couples no longer feel the need to have many children in order to ensure that at least some of them survive to adulthood. Added to this are similar improvements in both methods and knowledge of contraception (back in the day, the word 'prophylactic' would perhaps have been thought to be referring to a Professor Philip Lactic), and an increase in the average age of mothers when they give birth, with associated implications for fertility and the time available for bearing multiple children.

As ever with averages, there have been outliers. Clearly no couple can have fewer children than zero, but at the other end of the scale the sky has been, if not the limit, certainly a decent target at which to aim. John and Mary Thomas of Chester began having children in 1839 – a pair of twins – and didn't let up until they'd had 33, including a scarcely conceivable 15 pairs of boy–girl twins. As was sadly the case in those days, however, only a dozen of those children reached adulthood. Even so, Mary Thomas must have been a formidable multitasker (not to mention more sleep deprived than anyone outside a CIA resistance-to-interrogation module).

In 1895, Septimus and Jane Hill began a family that would run to 22 children, two of whom became notorious London criminals: Maggie, born in 1898, who was part of the Forty Elephants shoplifting gang between the wars; and one of her younger brothers, Billy (born 1911), who became arguably the most powerful figure in London's underworld.

The Forty Elephants was an all-female gang operating out of the Elephant and Castle area of south London. (It is widely but incorrectly assumed that the name of the area comes from a corruption of La Infanta de Castilla, the title given to certain Spanish princesses, such as Catherine of Aragon. In fact, the name almost certainly comes from the presence of a cutler, whose Worshipful Company's crest features an elephant with a castle on its back, as a nod to the use of elephant ivory in cutlery handles.) They would raid shopping centres, hiding as many stolen goods as possible in clothing that had been specially modified with hidden pockets and extra capacity, and relying on the reluctance of store staff to search female customers. When London shops finally wised up to their tactics, they simply expanded further afield to provincial towns, dropping empty suitcases at left luggage on arrival and filling them on the return journey. Nowadays they'd be subject of Twitter police warnings and endless internet memes.

Billy Hill made his first fortune running black markets in the Second World War. After the war he branched out into West End protection rackets, and was also a burglar par excellence, graduating from smash-and-grab raids on jewellers and furriers to complex heists, such as the 1952 Eastcastle Street postal van robbery, which netted his gang £287,000 (the equivalent of about £8.8 million today, according to the ONS long-run prices series) and was at the time the largest robbery in British history. Neither Hill nor any of his fellow robbers were ever caught, despite huge amounts of official resources being poured into the investigation: more than 1,000 police officers assigned to the case, the postmaster general required to report to Parliament, and Winston Churchill himself demanding daily updates. Nowadays, the criminal activities of such characters, at least in England and Wales, and as they affect households rather than businesses, are measured by the ONS, which took over from the Home Office after a 2011 review. Despite concern over some types of violent but relatively uncommon offences (for example, police records suggested offences involving knives or sharp instruments increased by 7 per cent in 2019), the survey shows the overall level of crime has actually been broadly stable in the last few years. Of course, there have been changes in the sorts of crime experienced: domestic burglary is now much less common than before the turn of the millennium, while the spread of the internet has made us more vulnerable to hacking and viruses – according to the ONS survey, households experienced 376,000 incidents involving computer viruses and 540,000 involving hacking in 2019.

More recently (and less criminally), the world's first set of all-female sextuplets made their inaugural census appearance in 1991 (though, of course, under the confidentiality rules, that particular census return will remain closed till 2091). As was widely reported, Hannah, Luci, Ruth, Sarah, Kate and Jennie Walton had been born eight years earlier to Graham and Janet, a couple from Liverpool for whom this was their last attempt to have a baby after five years of trying and 13 rounds of drugs. Was the ONS to record cliché use, surely the top two in Liverpool that year would have been 'be careful what you wish for' and variations on 'you wait five years for a baby and then six come along at once'. The odds against a successful sextuplet birth were 104 billion (about 14 times the global population) to one. (Liverpool fans may feel that you'd get roughly similar odds on Everton winning the Champions League.) Graham and Janet never dressed any of the girls the same. 'I wanted them to be individuals,' Janet said, 'and even when they started school and wore a uniform, I kept a basket of different hair bands and socks so each one should have their own colour.' School brought its own problems, of course, though mainly for anyone stuck behind them in the queue to see the teacher on parents' evenings.

ALL ON MY OWN

More and more of us in the UK are living alone. The number went up by 16 per cent to 7.7 million between 1997 and 2017, while the UK population increased by only 13 per cent. That figure is now at 7.9 million, and by 2039 the number of one-person households is projected to rise to 10.7 million. This rise isn't in any way even across age groups: quite the opposite. The number of people aged 25 to 44 living alone actually fell by 15 per cent over the period 1996–2020, but this was more than cancelled out by the 68 per cent rise in the number of 45–64-year-olds living on their own.

Why such a big increase? Partly due to the large number of children born in the 1960s who are now in this age group, but also due to the fact that more people in this age group are divorced or single than before (13 per cent of 45–59-year-olds are previously married but no longer living as a couple, with another 12 per cent not living as a couple and never having married). Three-fifths of those who live alone are men, which is probably less down to their poor personal hygiene than the fact that more men than women never marry, that men tend to marry at an older age than women (and therefore by extension tend to marry women younger than themselves) and that women are more likely to receive custody of any children during divorce proceedings. Only above 65 is the pattern reversed and more women live alone than men (since women have higher life expectancy, there are more widows than widowers).

Figures from before the pandemic – which of course disrupted spending patterns along with so much else – suggest that people between 25 and 64 living on their own spent an average of 92 per cent of their disposable income, compared with two-adult households, which spent only 83 per cent of theirs (partly because solo dwellers have no-one with whom to share the costs of living, not just rent or mortgage payments but utilities bills and council tax liabilities too). They felt less financially secure, not least as a result of spending more of their income on housing costs, bills and food. Around half (51 per cent) of those who live alone said they always or mostly have money left over at the end of the week or month, compared with nearly two-thirds (64 per cent) of those who live with their partner. Slightly more than a third of those living alone said they wouldn't be able to make ends meet for more than a month, compared with 14 per cent of couples without children. Those who live alone are more likely to be renting, which in itself may be connected to a lack of financial security or the two may be connected, of course: renters can't accumulate wealth in the way homeowners can through equity in a home or paying off a mortgage.

The financial costs of living independently may explain why the number of younger people living alone is falling ('younger people' here meaning the lower half of the 25–64 cohort, i.e. those aged 25–44, and if you call a 44-year-old a 'younger person', they'll love you for evermore). In this respect, it's surely no coincidence that London has the lowest proportion of one-person households (less than a quarter) and Scotland the highest (more than a third), given the vast differences in house prices and rental rates between the two.

Solo dwellers are less happy and more anxious, consistently scoring lowest on the four main well-being questions that the ONS started asking a few years ago in its household surveys ('How satisfied are you with your life nowadays?', 'To what extent do you feel the things you do in your life are worthwhile?', 'How happy did you feel yesterday?' and 'How anxious did you feel yesterday?' Even reading those questions might be enough to make some people question their own well-being: and of course, as so often, correlation does not equal causation, and it may be that the circumstances that have led some people to live alone are having as much if not more of an effect on their happiness as the simple fact of actually living alone). On the other hand, they have fewer arguments about what to watch on Netflix, whose turn it is to put the bins out and why the hell the bath is so filthy.

The irony of all this is clear: that although living alone is by definition an individual, solitary, even private matter, it is not just an increasingly common condition but also, by extension, an increasingly communal one. Nor is it as simple as it seems. On the one hand, living alone can be presented as a bad thing, a sign of social fragmentation and selfish individualism. On the other, it wouldn't be possible – certainly not in such large numbers – without the security afforded by advanced modern states: the economic prosperity that means that at least some people can afford to live alone, the reliability of public services to enable soloists to function without the kind of more informal networks seen in less developed economies, medical advances allowing even people who would previously have been considered very old to live safely by themselves, and the communications revolution that allows people to stay in touch with family, friends and colleagues all around the world without ever leaving home.

POPULATION

The number of children per marriage may have been in long-term decline, but the number of the population as a whole has been on the up pretty much without pause over the two centuries of the census; not just more children making it to adulthood, but adults living increasingly longer, and of course rising immigration figures. The population at the time of the first census in 1801 was 10.5 million; 50 years later, in the year of the Great Exhibition and amidst national pride that the British Empire was the pre-eminent power in the world, the population had doubled to 21.2 million. In particular, an increase in two categories gave cause to be optimistic about continued imperial hegemony. The number of men between 20 and 40 – that is, of fighting age – had grown from 2 million in 1821 to 3.2 million, and the number of women in the same age bracket – that is, of marriageable and child-bearing age – had grown from 2.2 million to 3.4 million, with the implicit provision of young men and women, who a few decades hence would either be off patrolling far-flung corners of the dominions in three-piece suits despite infernal heat or themselves giving birth and repeating the cycle, as though the census was an exercise in brood mares and cattle rather than human beings.

As ever, the bald figures concealed some alarming inequalities regarding region and class. Fewer than half of Liverpool's children reached the age of 20, whereas in Surrey it was more than two-thirds (and life expectancy in the latter was 52, substantially higher than the national average of 40, let alone the much lower ones in deprived areas). The greater spread of disease in such areas had effects beyond merely life expectancy. The 1851 census showed that one person in every 979 was blind, mainly though by no means exclusively because of smallpox.

RELIGION

Questions of religion bring out the inner Jane Austen in us all, redolent as they are of both sensibility and prejudice (perhaps less so of sense and pride). For some years these questions weren't asked at all, but the past two censuses have introduced at least simple (if voluntary) queries about the respondent's religious leanings (or lack of them).

33.2 million people, or 60 per cent of the population, described themselves in 2011 as 'Christian', which may be news to those bemoaning falling attendances in church (and indeed to the vicars and priests who may feel that their sermons are falling not on deaf ears but invisible ones). Then again, the proportion is definitely falling: in 2001 it had been 71.7 per cent. In order, the next most popular religions were Islam (up from 3 per cent to 4.8 per cent), Hinduism (1.5 per cent), Sikhism, Judaism and Buddhism (less than 1 per cent each). But just as 'extras' can often score higher than many batsmen in a cricket innings, so too can an absence of religion, and/or a refusal to answer the question rank higher than some religions: 25 per cent of people gave no affiliation, and 7.2 per cent of people did not answer the question (it was the only voluntary question in the census).

Exactly 176,632 Britons claimed to be Jedi knights, and therefore presumably found the 25 per cent's lack of faith disturbing. (History does not relate how many of those 176,632 (a) kept droids in their house and (b) told the census takers that these were not, in fact, the droids they were looking for.) Not that this was all good news for the Jedi community: in 2001 they had boasted 390,127 adherents, more than double the total a decade later and at the time the fourth largest faith in the United Kingdom. Since the census did not extend to Tatooine, where the Jedis would presumably have constituted a sizeable proportion of the population (indeed, the idea of a desert planet is a hard one to compute in a country whose largest tract of sand is probably Clacton Sands), it was left to Brighton to act as Jedi HQ, with our becloaked friends accounting for more than 2.6 per cent of the town's population. According to press reports, in Scotland eight Strathclyde police officers had previously declared themselves Jedi, secure in the knowledge that the force was quite literally with them.

There are also correlations between religious affiliation and other beliefs. ONS statistics from 2018 show that 60 per cent of Sikhs and 55 per cent of Muslims consider political beliefs important to their sense of identity, though only a quarter of Sikhs had participated in political activities* during the previous year (compared with, say, 62 per cent of Jews). Volunteering was also higher among Jews (44 per cent) than any other religion. 71 per cent of Muslims felt a sense of belonging to their neighbourhood, but only a quarter of them agreed that many of the people in their neighbourhood could be trusted. (This in itself is perhaps the

---

* Political activities here being defined as: contacting a local official such as a local councillor, Member of Parliament (MP), government official, mayor or public official; attending a public meeting or rally, or taking part in a public demonstration or protest; signing a paper petition, or online or e-petition. Inexplicably, writing a stiffly worded letter to the editor of *The Times* and/or putting the world to rights over several pints with Derek in The Fox and Hounds did not make the cut.

most British thing imaginable: where would the makers of net curtains be without it?)

NATIONALITY AND ETHNICITY

The British Isles have always been something of a melting pot of different tribes, nationalities and ethnic groupings: those who come from overseas to live and work here for a short or long time, and who in census terms happen to be here on the one day a decade in which the count is taken. As far back as the Roman Empire, a grieving widower called Barates set up a tombstone for his late wife in what is now South Shields. His wife, Regina, was 'a Catuvellaunian by tribe', so came from what is now south-east England, but he himself was from Palmyra in what is now Syria. Mostly the inscription is in Latin, but his final sorrowful expression, 'alas', is in his native Palmyrene. It is impossible to measure how many Angles, Saxons and Jutes (to take Bede's description of the fifth-century AD incomers) there were, and likewise how many Normans (themselves essentially Vikings who'd learned French) came over in the wake of 1066; but these events helped forge a new nation.

By the nineteenth century, numerical records are easier to come by, at least as far as nationality is concerned. Writing of the 1861 census, Registrar General George Graham said that:

in the midst of 19,982,623 British subjects [in England and Wales] lived 84,090 subjects of Foreign States. They are of all ages; but there is a great excess of men between the ages of 20 and 40. 9,502 of the subjects of Foreign States belonged to America, 518 to Africa, 358 to Asia, and 73,434 to Europe; 40,909 of them are in London, and the rest are distributed all over England ... Of the subjects of France, 12,989 are reckoned, including teachers of languages, governesses, cooks, servants, merchants, clerks, seamen (1,532), tailors, bootmakers, dressmakers, and smaller numbers in a great variety of occupations. Italy sends us musicians, artists, priests, figure and image makers, looking-glass makers, and merchants. 667 Italian seamen were in our ports. Germany, with Austria and Prussia, besides seamen (4624), supplies us with a large number of musicians, teachers of the German language, servants, merchants, factors, and commercial clerks, watch and clock makers (965),

engine and machine makers, tailors, shoemakers;
with many bakers, and a large colony of sugar
refiners (1345). The cities, and especially the
metropolis, are the principal seats of foreign
residents. London in 1851 contained 30,057 persons
born in Foreign Parts; and in 1861 it contained
48,390 foreigners by birth.

Aside from the archaic and to our eyes easily lampoonable reference to 'Foreign Parts', what's also striking about this passage is the extent to which it both bears out and reinforces national stereotypes. Cuisine and fashion are the preserve of the French, the Italians take care of music and art, and engineering and clerking are of course strictly and efficiently Teutonic concerns. Almost a century before the Treaty of Rome established what was then the European Economic Community, here's a forerunner of the old joke that in heaven the French are the cooks, the Italians the lovers and the Germans the engineers, but in hell the Germans are the cooks, the French the engineers and the Italians organise everything.

Interestingly, it does not mention waiters as among the jobs often done by Germans, but it seems that in the late nineteenth century the number of German waiters rose, so that as one academic finds from the 1911 census: 'in 1911 about ten per cent of waiters and waitresses in catering employment in London were German and [they] also worked in cities throughout the country so that waiting had become the third most important occupation amongst Germans in Lancashire'. Even before 1914, hostility to them had become evident from the formation of the Loyal British Waiters Society in 1910, with 1,625 members at its inception. *Plus ça change* ...

In recent years there has been a similar growth in the number of overseas workers, many of them from the eight eastern Europe countries that joined the EU in 2004. That year, there were only 75,000 citizens of those countries working in the UK; by 2016, the year of the Brexit vote, it was over a million. Since then it has declined again, to 784,000 in 2021, though the total number of EU workers in the UK has changed little since the referendum.

The years since the Second World War in particular have also seen a dramatic shift in the ethnic composition of the UK. Of course, it is clear that people from different cultures have long come to the British Isles and settled here, and not just Barates the Palmyrene. This was most dramatically seen, perhaps, with the arrival of Germanic settlers at the end of the Roman occupation, a process that led ultimately to the creation of a new nation, England, with its own new language emerging much enriched by the French words the Normans later brought with them in 1066.

And people have always come from further afield, too: one of the salvage divers who worked on the *Mary Rose* immediately after she sank in 1545 was Jacques Francis, originally a pearl diver from an island off the coast of west Africa. When a pirate ship, the *Barbary*, put into Dover harbour on Christmas Eve 1615 seeking amnesty, the crew were dispersed to their home towns, mostly Plymouth, Bristol or London, as the state papers record. They mostly had English names: Hill (the captain), a Swift, two Fletchers and even one John Thomas; but two people stand out: 'Juda the Jewe' and 'Hamett the Turke' (by which the scribe probably meant that he was a Muslim). These two men must have joined the crew while they were operating from a Moroccan port, but Juda might well have been of Spanish descent, as many Jews had recently fled from Spain to Morocco, no doubt actually expecting the Spanish Inquisition (Monty Python's claims to the contrary notwithstanding). Unlike the rest of the crew, they will have had no original home in England, so it seems likely they ended up in London.

Indeed, our great port cities in particular have long played host to various ethnic minority communities, hardly surprising once Britain became the world's leading maritime nation, with trade routes, and an empire, all round the world. The beginning of large-scale migration from the Commonwealth is normally taken as beginning with the arrival from Jamaica of the *Empire Windrush* in 1948 in Tilbury, while other communities followed from other former parts of the empire. For centuries before this, we can catch glimpses of individuals from other backgrounds. To take two or three examples almost at random, in the eighteenth century Dido Elizabeth Belle, the daughter of a British naval officer and a West Indian slave, lived with her uncle the Earl of Mansfield at Kenwood House, and was famously painted alongside her cousin Lady Elizabeth Murray. And the splendidly-named Scipio Africanus Mussabini, though born in London in 1867, was of a mix of Arabic, Turkish, Italian and French ancestry. More usually known as Sam, he became an athletics coach and helped train Harold Abrahams to win gold at the 1924 Olympics – an event which will be familiar to all those who have ever gone jogging with the theme tune from *Chariots of Fire* playing on their personal stereos. The 1921 Census found Dr Harold Moody residing in Peckham, south-east London, one of 1,712 Jamaican-born people then living in England and Wales. Later he became a prominent campaigner for the rights of black people.

However, for many years official statistics did not fully capture the increasing diversity of population to which population movements were giving rise: the ethnicity question was not introduced into the census until 1991. Before this, there were, of course, questions asking about one's country of birth, but this had its limitations – it simply picks up anyone born abroad, whatever their citizenship or parents' background, as in the example above of Dr Moody. Boris Johnson falls among these, for example, having been born in New York in 1964. Nonetheless, with these caveats, it is clear that the proportion of the population born abroad has been rising, something one might perhaps expect given the changes the world has seen. In 1951, before the age of the jetliner,* 19 out of 20 people in England and Wales had been born in the UK; by 2011, when

---

* Yes, I know the de Havilland Comet first flew in 1949, but it didn't enter service until 1952.

over 69 million passengers travelled through Heathrow alone, that was down to just over 17 out of 20. As the world has globalised, the numbers of people both coming to live in the UK and leaving it for elsewhere have risen: in 1964, 211,000 people arrived and 271,000 left, for a net loss of 60,000 people; in 2019, the last year before the pandemic disrupted international travel along with so many other aspects of our lives, 681,000 people arrived and 409,000 left, leading to a net gain of 271,000 inhabitants.

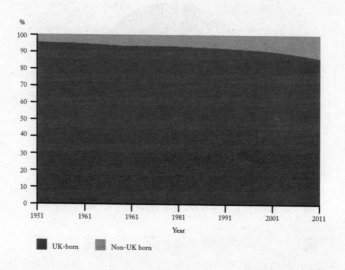

Figure 6: Proportion of the population of England and Wales born in the UK or abroad, 1951–2011
Source: Office for National Statistics

The census can, moreover, shed light on the circumstances of the so-called 'Windrush generation' – people who arrived from Commonwealth countries many years ago and who do not have documentation confirming their immigration status. These people faced difficulties in proving their right to work, to rent property and to access benefits and services to which they are entitled, leading the Government to apologise to them in 2018. Analysis of 2011 England and Wales

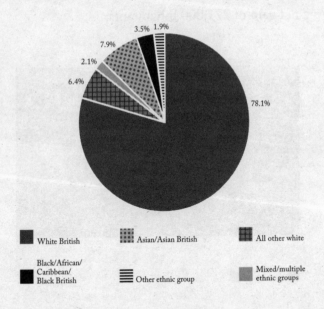

Figure 7: Population of England and Wales by ethnic group, 2019

Source: Office for National Statistics

census data was able to show that there were then about 120,000 people usually resident who had arrived before 1988 from the countries covered by the Windrush Scheme who did not have a UK passport, compared with about 1.1 million who did.

We will of course get an update from the 2021 census of how the current population is composed, but currently the most recent population estimates that the ONS has made for the different ethnic groups in the population of England and Wales relate to 2019. At that time, of the total population of 59.6 million, 78.1 per cent were white British; another 6.5 per cent white 'other'; 7.9 per cent Asian or Asian British; 3.5 per cent Black, African, Caribbean or Black British; 2.1 per cent from mixed or multiple ethnic groups; and 1.9 per cent from other groups.

LANGUAGES

The 2011 census included questions on the respond-ents' language; not in a maternal 'wash your mouth out with soap' kind of way, but in terms of one's main language and/or proficiency in spoken English. (The fact that the answer to the first question can be 'English' does not necessarily guarantee the second, particularly when alcohol has been taken and one is trying to explain oneself to the local constabulary.) English was the main language for 92 per cent (49.8 million), and of the remaining 8 per cent (4.2 million) who had a different main language, 3.3 million of those could speak English well or very well.

Clearly the fact that English is the default lingua franca of the world helps here. Of the top 10 main spoken languages other than English with the highest proportions who could speak English well or very well, four were native to countries where English was an official language (Afrikaans, Filipino, Shona and Welsh)* and the remaining six were Nordic or Germanic and native to countries where English-language learning is compulsory at school (Danish, Dutch, Finnish, German, Norwegian and Swedish). Again, this will come as no surprise to anyone who interacts regularly with northern Europeans and finds it a little shaming how they often speak better English than we do, or who has overheard waiters in Venice

---

* Whereas in England the census question on proficiency in English was asked of all those who did not have English as their first language, in Wales it was asked of those who had neither English nor Welsh as their first language.

taking the orders from their Japanese patrons in English.

At the other end of the scale, the main languages with the lowest proportion of those also proficient in English were gypsy/traveller languages, Romani languages, Pakistani Pahari (with Mirpuri and Potwari), Vietnamese, Cantonese Chinese, Yiddish, Panjabi, Bengali (with Sylheti and Chatgaya), Turkish and Latvian. This is almost certainly a reflection not just of cultural isolation but also linguistic distance, the measure of how different one language is from another. In terms of word roots, grammatical construction, recognisable vocabulary and so on, there are greater similarities between English and Nordic/Germanic languages than there are between English and Asian languages.

The most recent census also found that 562,000 people in Wales said they could speak Welsh – that was about 19 per cent of the population overall – but an ability to speak *Iaith y Nefoedd** was not evenly spread across the country, ranging from just 8 per cent in Blaenau Gwent to 65 per cent in Gwynedd. This was all much higher than the proportion of people in Scotland who can speak Gaelic: just above 1 per cent,

---

* The language of Heaven, for all you *pobl Saes* out there.

according to the census there. The findings of successive censuses also suggest that the proportion of people in Wales who can speak Welsh has roughly stabilised following a considerable decline during much of the twentieth century – from about 39 per cent in 1921 and 26 per cent in 1961, it fell to about 19 per cent in 1981 and there, more or less, it has stayed ever since.

Leaving aside questions of proficiency, the question 'what is the second most common language in the UK after English?' is a staple of pub quizzes the country over. *Gratulacje jeśli masz rację* – or, as we say in Polish, 'congratulations if you got this one right'. The 2011 census showed that there were 546,174 Polish speakers in the UK, almost exactly double the next highest (Panjabi, with 273,231). Urdu, Bengali (with Sylheti and Chatgaya), Gujarati, Arabic, French, all Chinese languages, Portuguese and Spanish rounded out the top 10. (To return to proficiency for a moment, of these 10, it was the French speakers who were also most comfortable in English, with 94 per cent pronouncing themselves 'proficient': a statistic which may raise eyebrows among those who marvel at the way the French judges at Eurovision are the only ones not to give their results in English, or at the way French restaurant owners will often communicate solely by

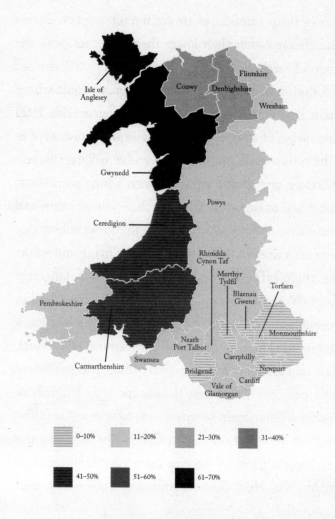

Figure 8: Welsh speakers in Wales
Source: Office for National Statistics

way of shrugs and elaborate arrangements of croissants and cheese rather than lower themselves to speak the lingo of *l'Albion perfide*.)

London had the lowest proportion of people whose main language was English at 78 per cent; not at all surprising, of course, given how culturally diverse it is. (The following is probably impossible to quantify, and therefore one should regard it with a little scepticism, but it was at one time thought that only London and Toronto could plausibly lay claim to having at least one person from every UN sovereign state living and working there.) The lowest proportion of first-language English speakers could be found in the London borough of Newham (58.6 per cent), while at the other end of the scale, Redcar and Cleveland in the North East had the highest proportion of English speakers at 99.3 per cent. In Wales, those reporting English or Welsh as their main language was lowest in Cardiff at 91.7 per cent and highest in Caerphilly with 99.1 per cent, which gives us the chance to wheel out an evergreen joke. How do you approach a Welsh cheese? Caerphilly.

Certain boroughs, towns or cities play host to large communities of one particular ethnic, religious or linguistic character. Three-quarters (3,000) of those who reported Yiddish as their main language lived in the London borough of Hackney and half (10,800) of those who reported Pakistani Pahari (with Mirpuri and Potwari) lived in Birmingham. Around a quarter (1,500) of those who reported Hebrew resided in Barnet and almost a quarter (300) of those who reported Krio resided in Southwark. Of those who reported Oceanic/Australian (any) as a main language, almost one in five (300) lived in Wiltshire.*

Slough had the highest proportion of Panjabi speakers (6.2 per cent), Leicester of Gujarati speakers (11.5 per cent) and Boston of Lithuanian speakers (2.8 per cent). Thanet saw the highest percentage of sign-language practitioners at 0.2 per cent.

---

* This clearly doesn't mean counting Australian English as a separate language, or else the proportions would be sky high in Southfields and Earl's Court, ah yeah good mate. That said, there are occasional differences between 'Australian' English and 'English' English so severe as to require translation. For example, former Australian wicketkeeper Ian Healy writes in his autobiography, 'Warnie's ripped one out of the rough and I've worn it', a sentence that in Northern Hemisphere parlance would read, 'Shane Warne turned a delivery so extravagantly out of the footmarks that I was unable to react in time and consequently received a blow to the face.'

THE DIGITAL REVOLUTION

Whatever questions John Rickman may or may not have considered asking during his years in charge of the early censuses, it's safe to say that those about internet access and the like were not among them. Indeed, such things would have seemed outlandish to census takers in 1971, let alone 1801. And yet here we are, living in a digital world, which has huge implications not just for the ways we live, which the census records, but also for the very nature and existence of the census itself. Rickman's entire rationale was that there were almost no useful data on the population whatsoever. Now there's scarcely a facet of our lives which is not and cannot be quantified, analysed and number-crunched. In just over two centuries we have gone from No Data to Big Data.

The fact that this book uses figures not just from censuses but also from ONS household surveys is in no small part due to the internet, which makes the collection and dissemination of such information so much easier than it would otherwise be. In 2020, 96 per cent of households had access to the internet (up 3 per cent from the previous year and up from 57 per cent in 2006), and 89 per cent of adults used the internet daily or almost every day (up 2 percentage points on the year and 54 since 2006). While almost all adults aged 16–44 years used the internet daily or almost every day (99 per cent for the 35–44s and 100 per cent for the younger groups), the older age groups used it less frequently: only 67 per cent of those aged 65 and over used the internet daily, while 18 per cent had not used the internet in the last three months. (This will come as no surprise to any middle-aged man or woman who has tried to set up video calls with elderly parents and then spent the next hour staring at their father's left nostril and the top of their mother's head.) For the first time more than half of those aged 65 and over shopped online, at 54 per cent in 2019, a figure which then rose sharply to 65 per cent in 2020, partly no doubt because of the lockdown. (This compares with the figure of 82 per cent for all adults, rising to 87 per cent in 2020). Almost half of all adults – 49 per cent, to be precise – make video or voice calls over the internet, a figure which has nearly trebled over the past decade. And in 2019 9 per cent

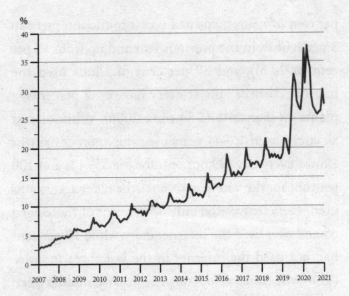

Figure 9: Percentage of retail sales in Great Britain via internet
Source: Office for National Statistics

of adults had encountered problems with fraud when
ordering things online in the previous 12 months.*

Naturally, the ONS has figures that help us chart the
rise of internet shopping, something that was a major,
perhaps even transformative, trend in retailing before

---

* I once received a call from my bank's fraud department asking if
I'd spent €800 on lager in a Calais hypermarket and £200 on body-
building products in Harrogate. I assured the caller that I hadn't,
but we both agreed that we'd like to go to a party held by whoever
had stolen my card details.

the coronavirus pandemic closed down many physical retail outlets in early 2020. The chart shows how the proportion of retail sales made online has been rising from less than 3 per cent in 2007 to over 20 per cent by the end of 2019. Interestingly, the sales seem to peak around Christmas each year before falling back a little, then resuming the general upwards trend. So the sort of things we buy each other as our pressies would often seem to be the sort of things we now go online for. Funnily enough, most years the peak actually came in November, not December, suggesting people are perhaps slightly uneasy about getting their last-minute shopping on the internet, in case it doesn't arrive by 25 December. The sudden, sharp jump in online sales in early 2020 is, of course, for a different reason – the coronavirus pandemic.

That said, different types of shop have seen different changes in patterns of shopping, at least in the run-up to the pandemic. Household goods stores saw the value of their internet sales go up less than threefold between 2009 and 2019, and predominantly food stores by little more; but textile, clothing and footwear stores saw almost fivefold internet sales growth, while non-store retailing (the category which includes the online-only retailers) saw internet sales up well over fivefold.

The way in which we use the internet is also changing. Partly this is technology: in 2019 84 per cent of people had used the internet 'on the go' (mostly through a smartphone), up a quarter since 2013. Adults looking for health-related information grew from 54 per cent in 2018 to 63 per cent in 2019 but oddly, in a year of global pandemic fell to 60 per cent in 2020, while those going on social networks grew to 70 per cent, up from 45 per cent in 2011. Reading online news rose to 70 per cent of adults in 2020, up from 66 per cent in 2019. (Perhaps wisely, no questions were asked about involvement in the unofficial tripartite pillars of the internet: cat videos, arguing about politics with total strangers on social media, and pornography.) Over three-quarters of people now use internet banking, up from barely two-fifths ten years previously (a rise which both fuels and is fuelled by the decline in high street banking).

London has the lowest proportion of internet non-users (3.9 per cent) while Northern Ireland continues to have the highest proportion (10.4 per cent). Like Asterix's village in ancient Gaul, the hold-outs are pretty steadfast. Of households without the internet, three-fifths felt they didn't need it, and a third also cited lack of skills and/or privacy and security concerns. But in an increasingly digital age, those who are not engaging effectively with the digital world are at risk of being left behind. Technological change means that digital skills are increasingly important for connecting with others, accessing information and services and meeting the changing demands of the workplace and economy. This is leading to a digital divide between those who have access to information and communications technology and those who do

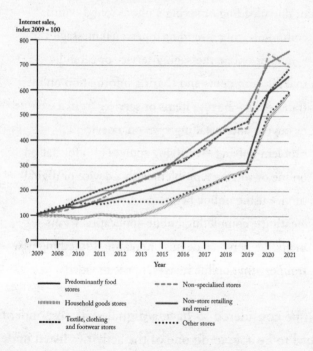

Figure 10: Internet sales in Great Britain by different store types
Source: Office for National Statistics

not, giving rise to inequalities in access to opportunities, knowledge, services and goods.

Government guidelines suggest that people should be able to perform basic digital skills in five separate areas:

- managing information – using a search engine to look for information, finding a website visited before, or downloading or saving a photo found online;
- communicating – sending a personal message via e-mail or online messaging service or carefully making comments and sharing information online;
- transacting – buying items or services from a website or buying and installing apps on a device;
- problem-solving – verifying sources of information online or solving a problem with a device or digital service using online help;
- creating – completing online application forms including personal details or creating something new from existing online images, music or video.

To be considered to have a digital skill, respondents need to be able to do one of the activities listed under it. As of 2018, according to the government guidelines, 8 per cent of people in the UK (4.3 million) were estimated to have zero basic digital skills (i.e. were unable to do any of the activities described in any of the five categories), and a further 12 per cent (6 million) were estimated to be missing at least one of those basic skills). Three-quarters of those with zero digital skills were over 65. For those who are partially or totally digitally excluded, the consequences can be wide-ranging, and again can be grouped into five areas:

- earnings benefits – increased earnings of between 3 per cent and 10 per cent through acquiring digital skills;
- employability benefits – improved chances of finding work for someone who is unemployed and an increased likelihood that someone who is inactive will look for work;
- retail transaction benefits – shopping online has been found to be 13 per cent cheaper on average than shopping in-store;
- communication benefits – allowing people to connect and communicate with family, friends and the community more frequently;
- time savings – around 30 minutes per transaction saved by accessing government services and banking online rather than in person. No queues, no

'Greensleeves' as hold music,* no customer in front of you who can't find the right paperwork …

Again, there are pronounced variations across the country here. In 2018, the South East had the highest proportion of people with all five basic digital skills (86 per cent) and the lowest proportion of those with zero basic digital skills (5 per cent), while the reverse was true for Wales (66 per cent and 19 per cent respectively).

EDUCATION, EDUCATION, EDUCATION

Some things in education never change. Concerns about class sizes and teachers' pay, for example, are as old as the hills. In 1900 there were on average 42 pupils per teacher, and the average teacher's salary was £128 for a man and £86 for a woman (or roughly £16,700 and £11,200 respectively at 2021 levels, again using the ONS long-run prices series to calculate the change).

---

* Dorset County Council used to have UB40's 'Rat in Mi Kitchen' as the hold music for their Pest Control Division, which was splendid.

Today's figures, by comparison, are a class size of 21.7 and median salaries of £41,168 for full-time male secondary teachers and £36,480 for their women counterparts.

But, in general, education is never static, and indeed never should be. Before 1918, the minimum school leaving age was 12; it increased to 14 that year, to 15 in 1947 and 16 in 1972. The education budget as a proportion of overall government spending has increased over the years, from 5.9 per cent in 1900 to 7.7 per cent in 1950 and 13.3 per cent in 2010. Tempting as it is to regard the subjects on offer during one's own school and university careers as the only 'proper' ones, with everything new that came afterwards pointlessly and uselessly trendy, both the popularity of subjects and indeed their very existence change over time.

The two decades between 1995 and 2015 show this. In 1995, there were fewer GCSEs and they were mainly in the core academic subjects. In the winners' column since then are all three sciences (physics, biology and chemistry) – good news for the UK's continued status as one of the world's premier scientific hubs – plus religious studies, Spanish, history and business studies. Less happy in the losers' corner have been French and

German (both of which more than halved in that period), English literature, art and design.

The respective fortunes of modern languages are particularly interesting. In general, languages are seen as relatively hard subjects in which to get good passes: in effect, you either know how to say or write something or you don't, whereas with, say, religious studies you can be a little more vague. Moreover, even a GCSE-level language won't make you anywhere near conversational in that language, let alone fluent. So if you are going to take a language, the thinking goes, it should be a useful one, and Spanish is now widely perceived as being more useful than French (it is, along with Mandarin, Hindi and English, one of the four most widely spoken languages in the world).

Ofqual statistics for 2021 reveal that the 10 most popular subjects for exams were combined science (840,955), maths (758,755), English language (729,605), English literature (572,765), history (278,880), geography (268,180), biology (171,835), chemistry (165,710) and French (125,655).

At A level, the most popular subjects in 2021 were maths (90,290), psychology (68,315), biology (63,765), chemistry (55,485), history (41,585), sociology (39,825), art and design (39,370), physics (37,560), English literature (36,135) and business studies (35,285). But those bald figures can belie the movements of subjects up and down the popularity tables. Geography, for instance, saw 16 per cent more pupils take it than they had done the previous year (up from 27,470 to 31,810), while both psychology and sociology saw 8 per cent increases on 2020. The biggest falling group between 2020 and 2021 was modern languages other than French, Spanish and German (down 17 per cent), followed by design and technology (down 9 per cent).

At university, the most popular subjects by application are – let's do this in reverse in order to instil a bit of ersatz *X Factor*-style tension:

10 Economics (67,560 applications in 2020)

9 Sport and exercise science (71,080)

8 Combinations within business and admin studies (80,815)

7 Design studies (89,715)

6 Management studies (92,590)

5 Pre-clinical medicine (102,240)

4 Computer science (103,345)

3 Law (129,480)

2 Psychology (139,405)

1 Nursing (229,555)

The choices are revealing for several reasons. First, they're all vocational. People still do go to university to study more traditional subjects, such as maths and humanities, but with tuition fees as high as they are, and the job market as competitive as it is, many students understandably feel that they should maximise their chances of employment. Second, many of those vocations are distinctly modern ones, or at least established ones with modern twists. Those who attended university in 1918 rather than 2018 would have been completely bewildered by computer science and not much less bewildered by sports science (this was an era when rowers trained for the Boat Race, a savagely brutal test of strength and endurance, by taking a brisk walk on the riverbank in a large coat followed by steak and port).* Law reflects our increasingly complex, litigious and rule-bound public life; psychology both the prevalence of mental health problems and the increased willingness to try to treat them. And nursing, as well as being truly vocational, offers a near guarantee of a job at the end, since the NHS

* When the future Field Marshal Lord Haig went to Brasenose College, Oxford, in 1880, the advice of its then principal, Dr Craddock, to his young undergraduates was to drink plenty of port and go out riding.

always seems to be seeking more nurses. Particularly notable is the increase in applications to study nursing, up 37 per cent in just two years.

LEISURE TIME

Men take more leisure time than women. Yes, that sound you can hear is the 33.65 million females in the UK asking you to tell them something they don't know. The gap is 40 minutes per day – six hours and nine minutes compared with five hours and 29 minutes respectively – though, as ever, this average masks huge regional variations: in the North West it's an hour a day and in Northern Ireland there's no gap whatsoever.

Unsurprisingly, ONS statistics from 2015 also found that men tended to spend their leisure time playing sports, practising hobbies, gaming and computing, or consuming mass media, while women used more time for socialising. And, when not at leisure, women were more likely to be performing unpaid work.*

---

* Unpaid work here describes activities that members of households perform for their own, or other, households for free, but that

Leisure time is lowest for those aged 25 to 34 (four hours and 46 minutes per day), but increases with age (those aged 65 and over spend seven hours and 10 minutes per day). Then again, since lots of those in that category had been to university relatively recently, perhaps it's about time they did some proper work. Those in skilled trades take the least leisure time while those in sales and customer service occupations take the most. Those employed full-time take the least leisure time but enjoy it most, and those from lower-income households are more likely to be working on weekends.

Both men and women spend the majority of their leisure time consuming mass media (watching TV, reading or listening to music). Men spend two hours and 21 minutes a day on this, as opposed to two hours and three minutes for women (a gap which can almost certainly be explained by the average man's 18-minute hiatus between 'Yeah, I'll be right up' and actually summoning up the energy to get off the sofa and go to bed).

---

could be contracted out to a market service provider. This may include activities such as childcare, adult care, volunteering or housework. At this point the male/female narrative is writing itself so easily that the author is going to the pub.

The British are also inveterate travellers, or at least have become so. In 1979, when the UK population was around 56 million (11 million fewer than now), there were 15.5 million trips abroad – in other words, one for every 3.6 residents. But with air-travel deregulation ushering in the age of the budget airline, that figure began to soar – 41.3 million in 1995, 53.9 million in 1999, 66.4 million in 2005, and by 2019 the original number had sextupled to 93.1 million, and in doing so had outstripped the population. In other words, there was well over one trip abroad for every person, on average – although thereafter foreign travel plunged because of the pandemic: it's estimated that in April to June 2021 UK residents made 95 per cent fewer air trips abroad than they had in the same period of 2019, due to the coronavirus pandemic.

And an increasing proportion of those were holidays rather than business travel. In both 1985 and 2000, around 15 per cent of trips taken abroad were business-related. But by 2019 that figure was down to 10 per cent, as e-mail, virtual conferencing and the like allowed business to be done remotely (and this figure will almost certainly continue to fall as a result of the coronavirus Zoom boom).

The number-one destination for Brits heading abroad is Spain, as it has been for most of this century: there were 18.1 million trips made in 2019. Second is France, with 10.3 million visits, which once held the crown but lost it to its neighbour across the Pyrenees, and third is Italy, with 5.1 million. All three offer a combination of cheap wine and sunshine, which is at least 80 per cent of what any self-respecting Brit wants in a holiday, followed by the USA, Ireland, Netherlands, Greece, Germany, Portugal, Poland,* Turkey, Belgium, India, Switzerland and the United Arab Emirates (mainly Dubai, which is visited around 800,000 times by Britons: more than 20 times the number in the mid-nineties). The ease and affordability of foreign travel is something we've taken for granted these past few decades – back in the fifties, a one-way ticket to the US with Trans World Airlines could cost more than £5,000 in today's money – but the extent to which this remains true in a post-coronavirus world remains to be seen. Certainly there may be countries that see fewer UK visitors than before, something which so far

---

* Not to take away from the charms of Krakow, but the high ranking of Poland can be partly explained by nationals of that country who live and work here returning home to see family and friends.

has been confined to destinations such as Egypt and Tunisia (largely due to security concerns).

As for domestic holidays within Great Britain, the good old seaside trip is still the most important, accounting for over two-fifths of nights away in those pre-pandemic days of 2019, according to the GB Tourism Survey from VisitBritain (though perhaps in some people's minds the word 'seaside' here is prefixed with the implicit 'sitting in a B&B looking out at a

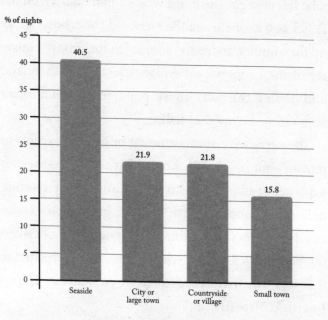

Figure 11: Domestic holidays – type of destination
Source: VisitBritain, GB Tourism Survey 2019

rain-lashed …'). Stays in cities or large towns or in the countryside or a village each accounted for just over a fifth of nights, while stays in small towns for just under a fifth. Interestingly, while seaside visits accounted for two-fifths of nights, they only made up a third of trips, fractionally behind trips to cities or large towns. So, when it comes to a mini-break, the city has it. As for which part of the country we go to, by far the most popular is the South West, surprising precisely no-one who has ever got stuck in a west-bound tailback on the A303 past Stonehenge the weekend the schools break up for summer. Indeed, it accounted for almost a quarter of the country's total nights away, with Scotland and Wales the next most popular, between them accounting for another half.

The popularity of caravanning or camping seems to remain – for holidays in England, it accounted for over a quarter of all nights, with other forms of self-catering making up another fifth (hotels, guest houses and B&Bs accounted for a third). The popularity of camping will shock all those who've agreed with the meme that says, 'My friends suggested we go camping. Things I need. 1. New friends.'

But, in the spirit of *Pointless*, what about our least visited countries? If one of the worst things about

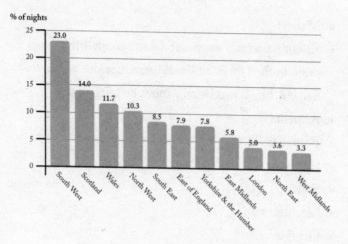

Figure 12: Domestic holidays – regions
Source: VisitBritain, GB Tourism Survey 2019

going abroad is the possibility of bumping into other Brits, where can you as good as guarantee not coming across someone with whom you'll have to make small talk, exchange e-mail addresses and then try to avoid upon returning home? Not Slovakia, Sri Lanka, Japan or Brazil, which each average more than 100,000 Britons per year. Not even Andorra, Tanzania, Bangladesh, Peru and Iran, which are all in the top 100. But these 10 see fewer than 2,000 Britons each year, or less than 0.003 per cent of the population:

- Malawi
- Kazakhstan (and no, Borat doesn't count. First, he came to the UK from Kazakhstan, not vice versa. Second, he's Kazakhstani. Third, he's fictional.)
- Armenia
- Botswana
- Uzbekistan
- Belize
- Liechtenstein
- Georgia
- Azerbaijan
- Mozambique

DEATH

THE DAYS OF OUR YEARS

A baby boy born in 2020 can expect to live, on average, 87.3 years: a baby girl can expect almost three years longer at 90.2 years, once you take into account expected improvements in mortality over their lifetimes. Either will take them well into the twenty-second century, by which time artificial enhancements will have rendered many of us transhuman, we will have colonised the Moon and Mars, and *Love Island* will be on its 200th series – for which see our final part, '2121: Back to the Future?' Of those babies, 13.6 per cent of the boys and 19.0 per cent of the girls can expect to live to 100 and get a greeting card from the queen or whoever the equivalent is by then (quite possibly even King George VII, who, being born in

2013, would need to live to be 107 to send centenary greetings to 2020 newborns – but he does come from a long-lived family).

If you're reading this having just retired at 65, you will (hopefully) be happy to know that you can expect 20 more years if you're a man, 22 years if you're a woman, and four months if you discover that being out of the house five days a week for the past four decades is all that's stopped your wife going genocidal on you so far.

But of course 65 these days is not what 65 used to be, as these figures show. For many years, 65 was the official pension age; indeed, the Germans set it there in 1916 (even though they might reasonably have been expected to have other things on their mind at the time, such as the senseless slaughter of their young men in the Great War). The UK followed suit in 1925, but interestingly – and this had been the case in Germany too – the decision to stick at 65 was actually a *reduction*. In both cases retirement age had initially been 70; the first British old-age pension had been paid out at that age in 1908 to 500,000 people, and had been set at five shillings. At the time only about one in four people even reached the age of 70 – the biblical 'days of our years' being three score and ten – and even the ones who did could not usually expect to make it to 80.* Nowadays, 65 is seen as too low for granting pensioner status, and the age is gradually being increased once more.

But what marks the start of actual old age? Part of the answer lies in looking at a population as a whole, measuring ageing by two increases: in the number and proportion of those aged 65 years and over, and in median age (the age at which half the population is younger and half older). On both of these measures, the population has aged and is projected to continue to do so. In 2020, there were 12.5 million people aged 65 or more, representing 19 per cent of the total population. Compare this both with halfway through the last century (in 1950 there were 5.3 million, accounting for 10.8 per cent of the population) and halfway through this century, by which time there are projected to be 17.9 million people of that age, making up 25.1 per cent of the total. The oldest old are the fastest-growing age group, with the numbers of those aged 85 years and over projected to double from 1.7 million in 2020 to 3.6 million by 2050 (5 per cent of the population).

* And, of course, the psalmist does warn that though men be so strong that they might come to fourscore years, 'yet is their strength then but labour and sorrow'.

In 1950 the median age was 34; today it's 40, and by 2050 it will be 43.

Another way of looking at old age is to find the point at which men and women have a certain number of years left, or remaining life expectancy (RLE). A 70-year-old man today has 15 years left, on average; a woman 17. In these terms, a man aged 70 today is equivalent to a man aged 65 in 1997, and a woman aged 70 is equivalent to a woman aged 65 in 1981. Just as strikingly, health seems to be improving across the

	Men (age at RLE 15)	Women (age at RLE 17)
1911	57.8	57.4
1951	59.0	60.6
1981	62.0	65.0
1997	65.0	66.8
2017	70.0	70.0
2037	72.9	72.3
2057	75.0	74.1

Table 1: Age at which remaining life expectancy is 15 for men and 17 for women, selected years, Great Britain

board at all ages, so a direct comparison is in general appropriate: that the increase in ageing has come with an increase in standards of health.

Life expectancy calculations are not just of academic interest: they're vital tools for policymakers in, for example, setting the state pension age or allocating resources to old-age care. (And of course to private providers too, such as health insurance/life insurance companies.) From an economic and societal point of view, longer lives mean people can continue to contribute for longer – through longer working lives, volunteering, and possibly providing care for family members, for example grandchildren. But more older people means increased demand for health and adult social services, and increased public spending on pensions. It's no accident that the Department for Work and Pensions lumps the two together, because neither can exist without the other.

NO-ONE GETS OUT OF HERE ALIVE

Death rates are running, as they always do, at 100 per cent – no-one gets out of here alive – but fewer people are dying every year than ever before, both in absolute and proportionate terms. In 1918 there were 715,246 deaths in the UK, compared with 616,014 in 2018, a decrease of about 14 per cent; but in that time the population rose by 67.8 per cent from 39.6 million to 66.4 million, making the 1918 death toll 18.1 per thousand of the population but the 2018 toll only 9.3 per thousand. Admittedly, 1918 was a very bad year for mortality, because of the Spanish flu pandemic, but even in 1913, just before the war, the death rate had been 14.1 per thousand. Repeat the calculation, comparing 1920 and 2020, and you get a rather different picture: the mortality rate only improves from 12.7 per thousand in 1920 to 10.2 in 2020. Of course, by 1920 the flu pandemic had passed and so the number of deaths had fallen, while 2020 saw deaths rise as COVID-19 struck, nearly a fifth higher than two years before.

Old people are dying in much greater numbers now, but only because people are living to old age in much greater numbers. Only 0.7 per cent of the population of England and Wales were aged 80 and over in 1918, compared with 5.0 per cent of the UK population in 2020. For the very young, the situation is mercifully totally different. In 1920, 92,185 children under the age of one died, compared with just 2,620 in 2020.

The main causes of death have mutated over time. Before 1945, infectious diseases were the leading cause of death for young and middle-aged people of both sexes. But childhood immunisation and the consequent virtual eradication of diseases such as diphtheria, measles, mumps, polio, rubella, tetanus and whooping cough have drastically reduced these numbers. The decline in infectious fatalities coincided with a rise in motor vehicle crashes, which really began to escalate during the Second World War (with vehicles obliged to drive in total darkness at night as part of the blackout) and only began to decline after seatbelts were made compulsory in 1983. Now young people are most likely to die from external causes (drug misuse, suicide and self-harm), while heart disease accounts for many older men and breast cancer for many middle-aged and older women.

Not all deaths are equal, of course. Many are effectively old age, the traditional 'good innings'; some are tragic, others anonymous. But a few have been downright bizarre. Here are a magnificently outlandish seven.

A 30-year-old Lincolnshire woman died from eating her own hair in 1869. The post-mortem uncovered a 2lb solid lump in her stomach. 'This remarkable concretion had caused great thickening and ulceration of the stomach, and was the remote cause of her death', said the *Liverpool Daily Post*.

In 1872, pallbearer Henry Taylor tripped during a funeral in Kensal Green cemetery, north-west London. His fall meant that the other pallbearers lost their grip on the coffin, which fell on to Henry himself and killed him. 'The greatest confusion was created amongst the mourners who witnessed the accident, said the *Illustrated Police New*, 'and the widow of the person about to be buried nearly went into hysterics'.

In 1875, a man accidentally swallowed a mouse while trying to catch it in a south London factory. 'That a mouse can exist for a considerable time without much air has long been a popular belief and was unfortunately proved to be a fact in the present instance,' said the *Manchester Evening News*, 'for the mouse began to tear and bite inside the man's throat and chest, and the result was that the unfortunate fellow died after a little time in horrible agony.'

'DEATH OF SIR WILLIAM PAYNE GALLWEY' hollered the *Northern Echo* on 20 December 1881: a headline that scarcely did justice to the story beneath. Payne Gallwey, a former MP, had been 'out shooting in the parish of Bagby, and in crossing a turnip field fell with his body on to a turnip, sustaining severe internal injuries. All that medical aid could do was done, but with Sir William's failing health he gradually sank, and died, as stated above, about ten o'clock yesterday morning.' Despite his death in surely the most bizarre shooting accident of all time, his son Ralph was not put off from the pastime, becoming the author of, among other must-read titles, *The Book of Duck Decoys: Their Construction, Management and History* and *Letters to Young Shooters*.

In August 1896, a car belonging to the Anglo-French Motor Carriage Company was being used to give demonstration rides at London's Crystal Palace. The car fatally hit 44-year-old Bridget Driscoll, making her the first recorded pedestrian to be killed in a collision with a car.

Thornton Jones, a lawyer in the Welsh town of Bangor, awoke one morning in 1924 to find that his throat had been slit. Unable for obvious reasons to speak, he wrote: 'I dreamt that I had done it. I awoke to find it true,' and died 80 minutes later. He had indeed slit his throat himself while unconscious, and the inquest delivered a verdict of 'suicide while temporarily insane'.

Basil Brown, a 48-year-old health food advocate from Croydon, died from liver damage in 1974. He'd drunk (38 litres) of carrot juice over the previous 10 days and consumed 70 million units of Vitamin A, around 10,000 times the recommended dose for an adult male. His skin had turned bright yellow.

More generally, what kills us varies. As is so often the case, the media make the rare seem routine and the routine seem rare. A look at the 2010 England and Wales figures, for example, show the following:

- 493,242 people died in all, 237,916 men and 255,326 women.
- 2,148 babies died before reaching the age of 28 days, 1,184 boys and 964 girls.
- Cancer accounted for 141,446 deaths (74,267 male and 67,179 female).
- 25,106 people died of dementia, an increase of 11 per cent on the previous year. More than two-thirds of those, 18,349, were women (partly because they live longer than men).
- Heart disease killed 40,721 men, accounting for 17 per cent of all male deaths.
- Almost two-thirds of the 19,916 who died from mental or behavioural disorders were women (13,617, as against 6,299 men).
- 11,438 people died in accidents, comprising 6,354 men and 5,084 women.

- 5,388 people committed suicide, more than three-quarters of them men.
- 3,649 people died in falls, split almost exactly 50–50 between men and women.
- 429 motorcyclists were killed, only 22 of whom were women.
- 237 people died in fires.
- 203 people died from choking on food.
- 188 people died from accidental alcohol poisoning, 130 of whom were men.
- 123 cyclists were killed, 97 of whom were men.
- 29 people drowned in the bath.
- Six people died from starvation.
- Five people died from being stung by hornets, wasps or bees.
- Three people, all female, died from being bitten by dogs.
- No-one died from being struck by lightning.

And not all days are created equal when it comes to death either. 6 January traditionally has the highest number of deaths of any day in the year, around 25 per cent more than usual: between 2005 and 2017 it averaged 1,732 deaths compared with the overall daily average of 1,387. (5 January and 7 January aren't much better either, in case you're wondering: they each come in at 1,729 deaths, just three fewer.) There are several possible reasons for this: there tend to be more deaths in winter anyway, especially if it is a bad year for flu; some old people are sustained by the excitement of Christmas with their families but go into a decline when it's over; fewer hospital staff are on duty over the festive period; and family and financial pressures lead to a spike in suicides. At the other end of the scale, 30 July is the least likely day for people to die, with just 1,208 deaths on average – 13 per cent lower than usual.

PART TWO

WHAT WE DO

Work is the stage on which most of us act out our lives. Quite apart from our tendency to define ourselves by our job (asking someone 'What are you?' at a party will more likely get an answer like accountant, teacher, landscape gardener or whatever it is that pays the bills, rather than stamp collector, guitarist, family historian or whatever it is that person really likes doing).

To the dismay of everyone who looked forward to the future 'leisure society' so erroneously predicted back in the sixties and seventies, more people were working at the start of this decade than ever before. In January–March 2020, just before the pandemic forced the economy into lockdown, the UK saw a record high employment rate of 76.6 per cent of the population aged between 16 and 64 (it fell to a trough of 74.6 per cent later in 2020 but recovered much of the lost ground in 2021). And, contrary to claims that this was driven by large numbers of people working very short hours, in fact only just over 1 per cent of workers usually work six hours or less a week, down from about

2 per cent in the early 1990s. Indeed, before the pandemic the average full-timer spent between 36 and 37 hours a week at work;* that's roughly a third of the time we're actually awake. Work is vital, too, to our paying our way – in 2014, on average, virtually two-thirds of household income came from employees' wages and salaries (the remainder coming from various other sources, such as social security benefits, pensions, self-employment and income from investments).

THE CHANGING LABOUR MARKET

A number of suspicions have hovered over the UK's official employment figures over the years. The most persistent was that the numbers are deliberately 'massaged' or manipulated to the benefit of the govern-ment of the day. This was strongest way back when the

---

* With the onset of the pandemic, that average dropped markedly: in April–June 2020, average weekly hours for those employed on a full-time basis fell to 30.6; of course, many of these would have been on furlough and so actually working zero hours, bringing the average down. Thereafter the average has largely, but not fully, recovered to pre-pandemic levels: in September–November 2021 it was 35.8 hours a week.

lead indicator was the number of people receiving unemployment benefits. Then people could be moved off into various training schemes and other shelters that would conveniently 'disappear' them from the official tally of the jobless as read out on the evening television news.

Today, employment and unemployment are measured according to agreed international standards, and the main vehicle used by the ONS is the Labour Force Survey, a sizeable field operation that interviews about 35,000 households every quarter, thought to be the largest regular household survey of any kind in the UK. The ONS gathers a wealth of information from this randomly selected and rotating sample of people. They find out not just whether they are employed or not but what work they do, how much of it and how much they get paid. They ask whether they have a contract ('zero-hours' contracts only became a 'thing' quite recently) and whether they would like to work more. This Rolls-Royce of a survey provides researchers with unmatched insight into the working lives of the British. But it also has its critics, who point out that the findings are delivered too slowly to provide really timely insights – especially in times of economic shock. Just in time for the 2020 pandemic, the ONS had started to draw on faster sources of data, including the latest digital tax information, which revealed the shocking scale of the economic impact as people dropped off payrolls in their hundreds of thousands and the equally astonishing speed with which the number of employees recovered in 2021. Prior to the introduction of the LFS in the late twentieth century, we didn't have a continuous source of such rich data, but of course the decennial censuses do record people's occupations (with some quirks, as we shall see).

In 1891 the proportion of the population aged 20 to 64 in the workforce, whether or not they actually had a job at the time (what the ONS would now elegantly term 'economically active'), was 63.5 per cent, but of course this was an average – it was 96.8 per cent for men and 33.4 per cent for women (much higher for single, widowed or divorced women than for married women, naturally). The overall rate didn't change much into the twentieth century, but with more women working after the Second World War, it crept up to 65.3 per cent in 1951 and 68.7 per cent in 1961. The current ONS series for economic activity for 16–64-year-olds stood at an average of 79.3 per cent in 2019, a record high. Economic activity then fell off a little during the pandemic, and it is too early to say what the effect on long-term trends will be. There are many reasons behind the varying movements in the labour market, but alongside vast shifts in technology, automation, globalisation and gender roles have come major legislative changes too:

- nineteenth century: education policy and the legalisation of trade unions;
- early twentieth century: the beginning of the modern welfare state and widening of educational opportunities;
- immediate post-war period: the establishment of an expanded welfare state;
- latter half of the twentieth century: the passing of significant legislation to tackle gender and racial discrimination and disadvantage;
- early twenty-first century: equalisation of the state pension age.

HOW JOBS WERE

The 1851 census, taken as it was in the year of the Great Exhibition, with British pre-eminence in the Industrial Revolution at its height, shows a fascinating array of occupations. For men, there were:

- 243,052 shoemakers
- 183,255 men in the army and navy
- 135,028 tailors
- 37,698 civil servants
- 35,423 hose (stocking) manufacturers
- 30,047 ministers, priests, religious teachers and students of divinity
- 22,383 physicians
- 18,422 lawyers
- 18,348 policemen
- 16,890 saddlers and harness makers
- 13,872 carriage makers
- 13,426 hatters
- 11,895 hairdressers and wigmakers
- 8,600 artists 'in the wide sense comprehending all who devote themselves to the fine arts; including, however, 4,915 painters, some of whom generally call themselves artists, but are often called by others drawing-masters'
- 7,765 gunsmiths, armourers, sword-cutlers and bayonet makers
- 4,948 engravers (a figure which would fall by a quarter to 3,715 a decade later – perhaps not unconnected with the rise in photography; see below)
- 4,539 glovers (not including silk-glove makers)
- 4,388 copperplate printers and engravers

- 3,819 patten* and clog makers
- 3,617 hosiers and haberdashers
- 2,971 architects ('many of whom are undoubtedly builders')
- 2,534 shawl manufacturers
- 2,340 umbrella, parasol and stick makers
- 2,164 rag gatherers and dealers
- 1,838 prison officers
- 1,510 furriers
- 45 professional photographers (a number which would rocket by more than 50 times to 2,634 a decade later)
- and one abecedarian, a freelance teacher of the alphabet: Magnus Jamieson from Lerwick in the Shetland Islands

And for women:

- 267,425 milliners or dressmakers
- 145,373 washerwomen, manglers and laundry-keepers
- 72,940 seamstresses or shirtmakers
- 31,418 shoemakers

---

* A protective wooden shoe, often used to keep people's clothes clear of the muck and mire.

- 30,076 hose (stocking) manufacturers
- 25,343 glovers
- 20,538 straw hat and bonnet makers
- 12,769 staymakers*
- 17,644 tailors
- 7,628 bonnet makers
- 4,793 cap makers
- 3,299 shawl manufacturers
- 1,959 furriers
- 1,797 umbrella, parasol and stick makers
- 1,081 rag gatherers and dealers

More than three-quarters of a million people (782,213, to be precise) – were employed in the hemp, flax and cotton industries, most of them in cotton mills. Just over a third as many – 265,198 – worked in the coal industry, 'either extracting it from the earth, distributing it amongst the consumers, or manufacturing it into coke and gas'. And there were 3,510 artificial flower-makers of both sexes.

The 1851 census suggests how dangerous certain types of work were. Just short of 8 per cent of adult

---

* Or corset makers, as they would be better known to us nowadays.

women were widows across the country, but this figure was more than doubled in plenty of port towns, where merchant seamen and fishermen were active: for example, 16.2 per cent in Falmouth, 16.4 per cent in Yarmouth and 16.6 per cent in Bristol. Indeed, even in the early twentieth century, more merchant seamen were dying in accidents at work than miners (1,396 in 1902, compared with 1,063 miners, 721 factory operatives and 431 railway servants). But a far higher share of widows than any port could muster came from Alston in Cumbria, surrounded by North Pennines moorland and miles from the sea. More than one in five adult women here were nonetheless widows, the highest proportion of any town in Britain, and surely not unconnected to the fact that 1,038 of the 1,765 men there were lead miners.

Not all the listed occupations as given to census-takers tell the full story, however. In 1861, there was only one executioner left in England: William Calcraft, who lived in Tower Hamlets with two Louisas: his wife and their granddaughter. Calcraft actually gave his occupation as 'shoemaker', his initial trade, on the grounds that there weren't enough executions needed every year to count that as a full-time job. His career as a hangman had begun in 1829 and would continue until 1874, by which time he had executed around 450 people, averaging out at less than one a month. He was an aficionado of the old-fashioned short-drop method, where the prisoner fell only three feet or so through the trapdoor and died of gradual asphyxiation, rather than the newer long drop, which breaks the prisoner's neck and is therefore regarded as more humane. Calcraft would often pull on a victim's legs or climb on their shoulders to try to speed up the process, perhaps in a bid to entertain the crowds (executions were public until 1868 and could attract 30,000 spectators keen to make a day of it). He had at least three sources of income: the prices he charged for his shoes, the stipend he received for his work as an executioner, and whatever he could make by selling sections of the rope used to hang his victims (usually between five shillings and £1 per inch). Several biographies of him were published during his life, the first of them an 1846 octavo pamphlet rather splendidly entitled *The Groans of the Gallows*.

And if you're wondering why there were so many seamstresses, billiard-markers and slaves in some censuses, that's partly because those were the descriptions of choice for prostitutes, professional sportsmen and suffragettes respectively. The first was

	1851 (000)	%	1861 (000)	%	1871 (000)	%
Professions:						
Law	32	0.4	34	0.4	39	0.4
Medicine	60	0.7	63	0.7	73	0.8
Education	95	1.0	116	1.2	135	1.3
Religion	31	0.4	39	0.4	44	0.4
Art and Amusement	25	0.3	29	0.3	47	0.4
Literature and Science	2	–	3	–	7	–
Commerce:						
Clerks, accountants, bankers	45	0.5	68	0.7	119	1.1
Public Administration	52	0.6	64	0.7	73	0.7
Trade/Wholesale/Retail	547	6.5	674	7.1	838	7.8

Table 2: Growth of 'middle-class' occupations in England and Wales, 1851–71 (as per cent of total population)

presumably rather to the weariness of real seamstresses, the second was to disguise the fact that sports clubs paid those sportsmen (which was in many cases illegal) and so pretended to employ them in billiard halls, and the third was a self-explanatory part of a wider protest campaign in the quest to have women granted the vote.

The 20 years between 1851 and 1871 show the growth of middle-class occupations and the role of domestic servants for those middle classes. Domestic service continued to grow for many decades afterwards: by 1911 it was the largest employer of women and girls, accounting for 28 per cent of all employed women (1.3 million) in England and Wales.

For those who gave their occupation as 'pedestrian', such as John Angers of Newcastle in 1881, the word was neither self-deprecating nor sardonic. Pedestrians walked long distances (1,000 miles in 1,000 hours was not unknown) or ran against each other in sprints, in either case for cash prizes, which were considerable at the time. Promenaders out for an evening stroll they were not. Indeed, by 1881 there were so many new types of job that a special dictionary was drawn up to help the census-takers distinguish their crutters from their spraggers and their whitsters from their oliver men.* In Spitalfields that year, 36 women's job titles

---

* Respectively, a mineworker who blasts rock, his colleague responsible for positioning small wooden props, someone who whitens clothes and a blacksmith using a foot-operated hammer.

	1851	1861	% Change	1871	% Change
Female:					
General Servants	575,162	644,271	+12.0	780,040	+21.1
Housekeepers	46,648	66,406	+42.4	140,836	+112.1
Cooks	44,009	77,822	+76.8	93,067	+19.6
Housemaids	49,885	102,462	+105.9	110,505	+7.8
Nursery maids	35,937	67,785	+88.6	74,491	+11.4
Laundry maids	–	4,040	–	4,538	+12.3
Total	**751,641**	**962,786**	**+28.1**	**1,204,477**	**+29.3**
Male:					
Indoor General	74,323	62,076	−16.5	68,369	+10.1
Grooms	15,257	21,396	+40.2	21,202	−0.9
Coachmen	7,030	11,897	+69.2	16,174	+36.0
Total	**96,610**	**95,369**	**−2.3**	**105,745**	**+10.9**

Table 3: Domestic service in England and Wales, 1851–71

appeared for the first time, including velvet-coat maker and paste fitter. In the same way today, the ONS still has to keep the Standard Occupational

Classification up to date – additions in recent years to the index include 'YouTuber', while the 2020 additions include 'dog sitter' and '3-D modeller' – of which more anon.

The scale of the Industrial Revolution, and its effects on agriculture, can clearly be seen by comparing the censuses of 1881 and 1901. In those two decades the number of agricultural labourers in England and Wales fell by over a quarter from 1,200,000 to 870,000, while the number of industrial labourers climbed sharply: railway workers practically doubling from 165,500 to 320,500, roadworkers up by three-quarters from 341,000 to 595,000, metalworkers up by more than half from 775,000 to 1,200,000 and mineworkers similarly from 610,000 to 937,000. The rise and fall of industry and agriculture was, of course, a self-feeding circle: the more machinery produced, the more agricultural labourers found their jobs being outsourced to exactly that machinery, thus obliging many of them to retrain as factory rather than farm workers.

In 1851, the three largest categories of occupation were manufacturing at 39 per cent; services (e.g. transport workers, domestic servants; professional people – doctors, teachers, lawyers, etc.; those in banking and insurance; and retailers) at 25 per cent; and

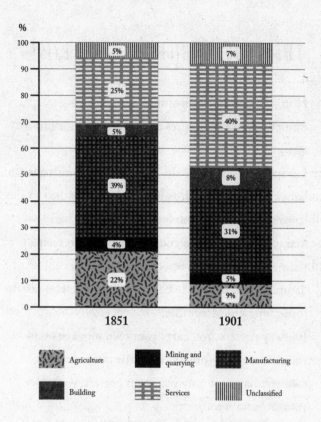

Figure 13: Occupational groups 1851–1901
Source: Office for National Statistics

agriculture at 22 per cent). The gap between manufacturing and services narrowed after that, and services forged ahead for the first time in 1881. By 1901, services accounted for 40 per cent, manufacturing for 31 per cent and agriculture for only 9 per cent.

TWENTY JOBS WHICH NO LONGER EXIST

1. Hop stringers: men on stilts would make a framework of poles, wires and strings for hops to grow.

2. Lamplighters, who would light and extinguish gas lamps in cities, though as late as the 1970s the lawyers' district of Temple in London still had manually lit gas lamps and a lamplighter to see to them. They are not to be confused with the 'lamplighters' in John le Carré's spy books, who do something else altogether.

3. Railway porters. You carry your own luggage on to trains these days (unless you're the queen, in which case you have not only your own porters, you've your own train too).

4. Pillow-lace makers.

5. Hot-stone newspaper printers. Newspaper pages would need to be made up using individual metal letters of varying sizes. It was one of the highest-paid unionised jobs.

6. Cotton mill workers. By the time of the 1911 census, the UK produced around 8 billon yards of cotton cloth, mainly from Lancashire, which

boasted around 2,650 mills employing 440,000 people. The First World War saw a loss of export opportunities and other countries setting up their own industries. By the time the Second World War began, 345,000 workers had left the industry and 800 mills had closed.

7. London Underground lift operators.

8. Traditional salt miners – there *is* still a salt mine in Cheshire, amazingly doubling as a document storage centre, but automation has replaced the old way of winning the salt with picks and gunpowder.

9. Costermongers: street sellers, of whom there were 30,000 in London alone. The journalist Henry Mayhew recorded the array of goods for sale: oysters, hot eels, pea soup, fried fish, pies and puddings, sheep's trotters, pickled whelks, gingerbread, baked potatoes, crumpets, cough-drops, street-ices, ginger beer, cocoa and peppermint water, as well as clothes, second-hand musical instruments, books, live birds and even birds' nests.

10. Mudlarks: usually children, who would wade thigh-deep in the Thames mud to retrieve anything they could sell, including rags (for making paper), driftwood (dried out for firewood), discarded cigar butts (recycled, amalgamated and sold as new) or

coins. Thames mud was not nice, pure and organic; instead it was a toxic morass of industrial and human effluent, and mudlarks could easily become stuck there or swept away by rising tides.

Mudlarking still goes on, of course – people have even made television series about it – but it's now more of a hobby than a profession, helped of course by the river being much cleaner today.

11. Pure finders. Exactly *not* what it sounds like. Pure finders collected dog faeces from the streets to sell on to tanners (the faeces were known as 'pure' because they were used to purify leather and make it more flexible). Some collectors wore a glove on their scooping hand: others figured it easier to keep a hand clean than a glove, and so went without.

12. Leech collectors. Usually poor rural women who'd stand in dirty ponds, wait for leeches to attach themselves to their legs, and then prise them off and sell them to pharmacies or doctors. The obvious 'yuck' factor of all this aside, leech collectors were at risk of catching nasty diseases from the stagnant water or losing too much blood from the leeches themselves.

13. Toshers. Sewer-hunters, who searched sewage for valuables that may have fallen through drain covers.

This was not just unpleasant work but actively
dangerous too: pockets of noxious fumes could be
fatal, tunnels could collapse, rats abounded, and a
suddenly opened sluice gate could knock a tosher
off their feet and drown them. Toshers were not
recorded in any census beyond 1841, as it had
become illegal the previous year to enter the sewers
without permission, but that didn't stop people
from doing it.

14. Matchstick makers. The white phosphorus on the
end of matchsticks was highly toxic, which
exacerbated the unpleasant conditions in which
matchstick makers (usually teenage girls) had to
work: long hours, cramped conditions, few breaks.
Since workers had to eat where they worked,
phosphorus often got into their food and could lead
to 'phossy jaw', a severely disfigured jawbone.*

* Female matchstick makers were responsible for a famous strike
in 1888 at the Bryant & May factory in London. Around 200
workers walked out in protest at the sacking of three of their
colleagues, who had spoken to social reformer Annie Besant about
their working conditions. Besant's article, 'White Slavery in
London', informed readers that 'the hour for commencing work is
6.30 in summer and 8 in winter; work concludes at 6 p.m. Half-an-
hour is allowed for breakfast and an hour for dinner. This long day
of work is performed by young girls, who have to stand the whole

15. Child chimney sweeps. An admonition beloved of
    modern-day parents to their children – 'in the
    olden days you'd have been up the chimney' –
    scarcely hints at how horrific this was: children as
    young as four sent scurrying up, knees and elbows
    rubbed raw, irreversible lung damage from smoke

---

of the time. A typical case is that of a girl of 16, a piece-worker; she
earns 4s. a week. Out of the earnings, 2s. is paid for the rent of one
room; the child lives on only bread-and-butter and tea, alike for
breakfast and dinner, but related with dancing eyes that once a
month she went to a meal where "you get coffee, and bread and
butter, and jam, and marmalade, and lots of it". The splendid salary
of 4s. is subject to deductions in the shape of fines; if the feet are
dirty, or the ground under the bench is left untidy, a fine of 3d. is
inflicted; for putting "burnts" – matches that have caught fire
during the work – on the bench 1s. has been forfeited, and one
unhappy girl was once fined 2s. 6d. for some unknown crime. If a
girl leaves four or five matches on her bench when she goes for a
fresh "frame" she is fined 3d., and in some departments a fine of 3d.
is inflicted for talking. If a girl is late she is shut out for "half the
day", that is for the morning six hours, and 5d. is deducted out of
her day's 8d. One girl was fined 1s. for letting the web twist round
a machine in the endeavor to save her fingers from being cut, and
was sharply told to take care of the machine, "never mind your
fingers". Another, who carried out the instructions and lost a finger
thereby, was left unsupported while she was helpless. The wage
covers the duty of submitting to an occasional blow from a fore-
man; one, who appears to be a gentleman of variable temper,
"clouts" them "when he is mad".'

and dust, deliberately malnourished to stunt their growth, sometimes burned by fires deliberately lit beneath them. As with toshers, 1840 was a watershed for sweeps – it became illegal for anyone under the age of 21 to climb and clean a chimney – but as with toshers, the practice still continued. It may tell you something about the attitudes of the time that there were 67 years between the formations of the Society for the Prevention of Cruelty to Animals (1824) and the Society for the Prevention of Cruelty to Children (1891).

16. Ratcatchers were pest control operatives and entrepreneurs all in one. They used dogs or ferrets to catch the rats, but instead of killing them they'd then sell them on to 'ratters', who'd promote a grisly spectator sport: inviting spectators (and wagers, obviously) to see how long it would take a terrier to kill all the rats. Perhaps the most famous Victorian ratcatcher was Jack Black,* who worked for Queen Victoria herself and used a cage that could store up to 1,000 live rats (as long as he fed them, that was; otherwise they'd turn on each other).

---

* Not the actor, though one can't help feeling this would be a good project for him.

17. Crossing sweepers. Children, usually, who would clear the filth from a small patch of street so that a rich man or woman could cross without getting their clothes or shoes dirty. In return, they'd receive a tip. Sometimes. It wasn't a great life, as anyone who remembers the crossing sweeper Jo from *Bleak House* will know.

18. Resurrectionists. Anatomists and medical schools could only officially get the cadavers of criminals who had been sentenced to death, so they always needed more bodies to dissect. Enter the bodysnatchers/grave-robbers/resurrectionists, who would dig up recently buried bodies and sell them on. Of course, from there it was but a small step (and some lateral thinking in terms of business development) to the antics of William Burke and William Hare, who murdered 16 people in 1827 and 1828 and sold the bodies on to Edinburgh University medical school. The Anatomy Act of 1832 gave doctors and anatomists greater access to cadavers, allowed people to leave their bodies to medical science and put an end to the resurrectionists' grisly trade.

19. Oakum pickers: unravelling lengths of tarred rope for re-use in caulking the seams in the hulls of

wooden ships. This was a particular favourite of workhouses.

20. Knocker-uppers hammered on doors or tapped bedroom windows with long poles to wake people up in the morning, until gradually put out of business after the mechanical alarm clock was invented in 1847. Parents of small children and cat owners will know the feeling of being subject to the whims of a living, breathing alarm clock.

HOW JOBS ARE

Our own concerns about the effects of automation on our employment patterns may be current, but they are not new, as the emergence of the Luddites in the early nineteenth century showed. Just as the Industrial Revolution superseded the agricultural one – William Blake's dark satanic mills asserting their supremacy over his green and pleasant land – so too have the technological and services revolutions superseded the industrial one. Today the services sector makes up more than three-quarters of national output and dominates the employment market, accounting for eight in every 10 workers. These services have ancillary effects too; for example, the plethora of mortgages on offer has helped contribute to ever greater rates of construction, and the 2011 census showed almost 8 per cent of workers employed in the building trade, the highest proportion on record.

By contrast, manufacturing these days accounts for less than 10 per cent of jobs, farming for less than 1 per cent (it had been 22 per cent in 1841 and 9 per cent in 1901). British farmers' contribution to economic output is only 0.7 per cent, the lowest figure in any G20 nation. As ever, the figures vary dramatically by region. The 2011 census showed that the Isles of Scilly went largest of anywhere on accommodation and food services (23.9 per cent of total employment), that Corby had the highest proportion of manufacturing jobs (23.7 per cent),* that Oxford had most people working in education (23.6 per cent), and that Kensington and Chelsea was estate-agent nirvana (3.4 per cent).

Around 3.6 million adults in the UK – getting on for 10 per cent of the working population – have never

* Disappointingly, the eponymous trouser press was named after the company founder John Corby, from Windsor, rather than its place of manufacture, so these people are unlikely to be making clever gadgets destined to reside permanently at the back of hotel-room wardrobes.

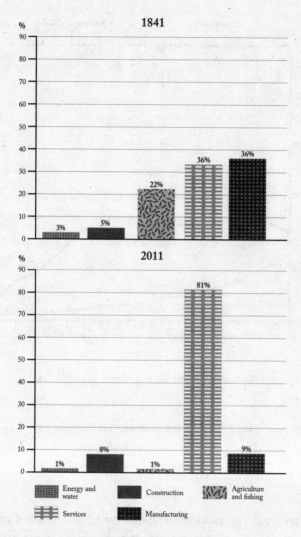

Figure 14: 170 years of industrial change across England and Wales
Source: Office for National Statistics

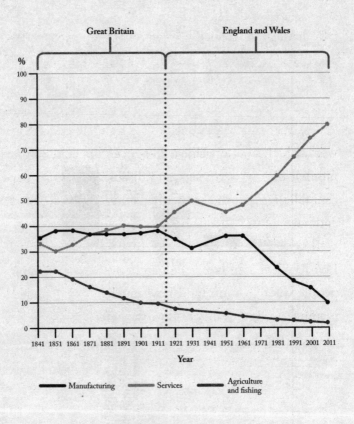

Figure 15: 170 years of industrial change across
England and Wales
Source: Office for National Statistics

been paid for work. The majority of these are those aged between 16 and 24 (71 per cent, including students), but even when those in full-time study are removed from the equation, more than half of those who have never carried out paid work are aged under 30. That 3.6 million represents a 270,000 increase on the figures from 2008, but 230,000 of those 270,000 are students: a 15 per cent increase in the number of 16–24-year-olds who are studying and yet to do paid work, which sits alongside a 23 per cent increase in the number of long-term sick and disabled, but a 28 per cent fall in those who are neither students nor disabled and have never had a paid job.

There's no easy way to say this: life disappoints. Don't believe it? Here's the gap between what young people wanted to do (and how much they envisaged earning) and the reality of how they ended up.

In 2016, the top five jobs that 16–21-year-olds wanted to do were, in order:

1. artistic, literary and media (e.g. writer, actor, movie director/producer)
2. teaching and educational
3. health professional (e.g. pharmacist, dentist, vet)
4. protective services (e.g. police office, firefighter)
5. nursing and midwifery

Incidentally, these were unchanged from the top five jobs being sought by the same age group in 2011.

But of those five, only one – teaching – ended up among the top 10 jobs actually done by 22–29-year-olds in 2017:

1. sales assistants and cashiers
2. caring personal services
3. teaching and education
4. sales and marketing
5. administrative
6. IT and telecommunications
7. childcare and related personal services
8. business, finance and related
9. customer service
10. construction and building

A quarter of those aged 16–21 felt that a high income was 'very important' to them, with only 15 per cent saying that it was not important. Half expected to earn £35,000 by the age of 30 with a degree and £25,000 without one; but the average salary of a 30-year-old is only £23,700. Five per cent thought they could earn £80,000 or more by the age of 30, though in reality only 2 per cent of 30-year-olds do so. Job satisfaction

(71 per cent) and security (60 per cent) were more important than a high income. The latter may reflect fears of being caught up in the gig economy, though in fact only 2.2 per cent of those aged 25–34 in employment were on zero-hour contracts in their main job in late summer 2019.

TEN NEW JOB CATEGORIES IN 2020

Roughly every ten years the ONS updates its Standard Occupational Classification, which it uses in many of its labour market statistics; and it has recently published the 2020 version. Here are some of the new work categories it now recognises, often where a job has become sufficiently important that it needs its own separate classification.

1. Cyber security professionals. Pretty self-explanatory in an age when never a week seems to go by without some news of a large firm getting its website hacked.
2. Teachers of English as a foreign language. Previously lumped in with 'teaching and other educational professionals not elsewhere classified',

but they're now a thing in their own right. Given the global popularity of English as a means of communication, that's hardly surprising.

3. Delivery drivers and couriers. Previously just lumped in with 'van drivers', all those people driving round all day delivering your online shopping are now recognised as belonging to an occupation all of its own.

4. Coffee-shop workers. Again now a category in their own right distinct from kitchen and catering assistants, the baristas are not to be confused with m'learned friends in the longer-established profession of barrister.

5. 3-D modeller. Seemingly nothing to do with 1:72 scale Spitfire propellers and polystyrene cement, more's the pity.

6. Data analysts. One wonders why the ONS of all people didn't have a separate category for this sooner.

7. Database administrators and web content technicians.

8. Charitable organisation managers and directors – in 2018, the Charity Commission reckoned that charities had a total annual income of £77 billion, so that would take some managing.

9. Dog walkers – finally recognised 83 years after George Gershwin wrote them their own theme tune.

10. Exam invigilators. Did we mention we'd be setting you a test when you've finished reading this book? No cheating!

WOMEN AT WORK THEN AND NOW

Employment patterns have changed significantly for women in the UK. The proportion of women who were in work in the 1850s, 1860s and 1870s appears to have been higher than any recorded again until after the Second World War. Certainly, the employment rate for women aged 20–64 fell from 33.4 per cent in 1891 to 30.7 per cent, before rising to 36.3 per cent by 1951. Family budget evidence suggests that around 30–40 per cent of working-class women contributed significantly to household incomes in the mid-Victorian years, and may even have been higher during the earlier decades of the Industrial Revolution, before the rise of state intervention regulating female labour (itself prompted by trade-union pressure) and promoting the ideal of the male breadwinner.

Domestic service of all kinds was the single largest employer of women: the 1851 census showed that this accounted for 50 per cent of employed women in London and 40 per cent in provincial cities. Next came the textile and clothing sectors, followed by metalwares, pottery, and petty trades such as confectionery, brewing, laundry work, cleaning and retailing.

For middle-class women in Victorian times, things were different, and to a much greater extent than their working-class counterparts, they were expected to be more involved in family and home life at the expense of paid work, and were placed on a pedestal of moral probity, motherhood and domestic orderliness.* This was the case for married women, of course, but there were caveats. Not only were they sometimes involved behind the scenes in family businesses (such as book-keeping and administrative tasks), but widows

---

* The differences in class attitudes persisted long after the Victorian era ended, and in some perhaps unexpected ways too. The 1945 movie *Brief Encounter* was a tearjerker for middle-class audiences beguiled by the tale of Alec and Laura, who embark on a passionate but unconsummated affair and are tortured by the social expectations placed on them as married middle-class people; but it reportedly played much less well among many working-class audiences, who didn't understand why the protagonists agonised so much rather than just jumping into bed together.

and spinsters needed to earn a living and could often be found as governesses, milliners, inn-keepers and grocers. It was not until 1870 that the Married Women's Property Act allowed wives to keep their own earnings rather than hand them over to their husbands. Even then it would be almost another 50 years until the 1919 Sex Disqualification (Removal) Act allowing women to become lawyers, vets and civil servants, and another 50 years beyond that before the 1970 Equal Pay Act came in following the strike two years previously of 187 women in the trim shop at Ford's Dagenham plant, a dispute famously celebrated in the 2010 film *Made in Dagenham*.

Women's employment changed significantly during the two world wars, and they played vital roles in war-related industries such as the production of ammunition. While 23.6 per cent of women were employed in 1914, this increased to 36 per cent in 1918. Indeed, right at the beginning of hostilities, the official *Board of Trade Labour Gazette* had speculated that the war could lead to higher unemployment through the disruption of the economy, not realising the huge demand for men of military age that the recruitment of the 'Kitchener Armies' would entail. The First World War helped change things for women in almost all aspects of work. The number of women in the civil service, for example, increased five times to almost 200,000, itself more than half of the total. Most of the new recruits were in support roles, such as clerks and typists, and though necessary according to the exigencies of the war, they were not altogether popular; a July 1915 letter to *Red Tape*, the Assistant Clerks' Association magazine, said 'it has not been demonstrated that the supply of unemployed men clerks whose services could have been obtained for a reasonable wage, had been exhausted'. Another correspondent described one of the temporary clerks who arrived at the office 'in all the glory of paint and powder, short skirts, high cloth boots, transparent blouses. She came – men saw – she conquered ... I have heard tell of men, formerly confirmed misogynists, who now sit surrounded by a bevy of beauty and find the official day all too short.' Shades of Zuleika Dobson (who, in Max Beerbohm's 1911 novel of that name, had given up being a governess for stage conjuring!).

The Second World War also brought a large increase in the number of women in both civilian employment and, of course, the armed forces. In July 1939 the number of men in the forces was already ramping up:

480,000, up 95,000 on the previous year. That total would peak at 4.65 million in 1945 before demobilisation started to bring it down. Meanwhile, the number of women in civilian employment went from 4.61 million in 1938 to peak at 6.77 million in 1943. Women also joined the services in large numbers with the establishment (or re-establishment) of the women's branches of the Navy, Army and Air Force. By 1944, 467,000 women were serving.

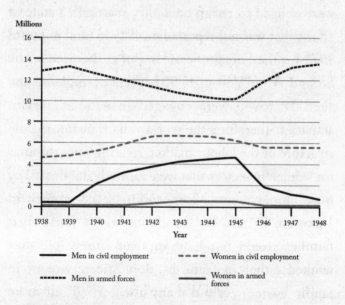

Figure 16: Men and women in civil employment and the Armed Forces 1938–48

Source: Office for National Statistics

Outside periods of war, women's position in the labour market was more marginal. A combination of explicit rules and social norms meant that women faced limited opportunities to work, and where work was available it was often less well paid. Though some of women's new-found status remained after the war, other aspects partially or totally reverted to the *status quo ante*; indeed, married women were prohibited from joining the civil service at all (and single women were obliged to resign once they married), a state of affairs that was not repealed until 1946 (and not until 1973 for the Foreign Service). But at the peak of the Second World War, up to 90 per cent of single women aged 18 to 40 were engaged in national service activities. Therefore, the world wars transformed the structure of the labour market, creating opportunities for women in sectors that were formerly dominated by male employment. Most working-class women in Victorian Britain had no choice but to work: their families would not have survived otherwise. They worked either in factories, domestic service or in family businesses, and many also carried out more informal home-based work, such as finishing garments and shoes, laundry, or making snacks to sell in the market or streets. (This was, of course, in addition to their unpaid work at home: cooking, cleaning, childcare and so on, without the assistance of modern labour-saving devices.)

Since the Second World War, the position of women in the labour market has changed radically. Industrial changes, incremental improvements in legislation and shifting social attitudes have all contributed to a significant increase in female participation in the labour market. Table 4 shows the number of women aged 16 years and over who were engaged in economic activity between 1951 and 2020 (in 10-year averages). It shows

Period	Number economically active women
1951 to 1960	6.91 million
1961 to 1970	8.35 million
1971 to 1980	10.12 million
1981 to 1990	11.7 million
1991 to 2000	12.72 million
2001 to 2010	13.99 million
2011 to 2020	15.51 million

Table 4: Number of economically active women over time in the UK, 1951–2020

that female economic activity increased more than doubled over the period of 1951 to 2020.

More women are employed now than at any time in recent history. In 1975, only 57 per cent of 'prime working age' women (that is, between the ages of 25 and 54) were employed, a figure which rose to a record high of 78 per cent in 2017. The proportion of mothers aged 24 to 54 in paid work has mirrored this rise almost exactly, up from 50 per cent in 1975 to 72 per cent in 2015. There are several reasons for these figures, but the most important ones are the greater levels of education and opportunities for women in the labour market, and the fact that women are having fewer children later in life and are therefore less likely to stop working permanently once they've become mothers. Only 41 per cent of women born in 1958 were still in work two years after the birth of their first child, but for those born in 1970 this figure was 58 per cent – even though both cohorts had the same employment rates for five years before and 10 years after the birth of their first child. The proportion of couples with children where only one adult works has almost halved (down from 47 per cent in 1975 to 27 per cent in 2015) and the proportion where both partners work has increased from 49 per cent to 68 per cent.

Women are also more likely to have never done paid work than men, particularly in older age groups. Among non-students aged between 25 and 64 years who have never had a paid job, more than 72 per cent are women. This is at least partly because women are far more likely to take on the bulk of childcare: of those who have never done paid work and are currently looking after the family or home, women account for 94 per cent, rising to 96 per cent in cases where there is a dependent child in the family. Full-time professional househusbands who have never worked do exist, clearly, and their numbers are slowly on the rise, but they still remain a small minority.

The gender pay gap among full-time employees stood at 7.9 per cent in 2021. It is coming down, but very slowly, falling only 1.6 percentage points since 2012. It is also concentrated very much amongst older workers: the gap is close to zero amongst workers under 40, but 12.3 per cent for those aged 40–49 and about the same for those over 50. The figure for 40–49-year-olds has decreased substantially over time, but not so for those over 50, which demonstrates that women are less likely to work in higher-paid jobs, such as managers, directors or senior officials.

Among all employees, not just full-time ones, the

gap was 15.4 per cent in 2021, reflecting that women tend to fill more part-time jobs where the median pay is lower, even on a per-hour basis. The largest gender pay gap among all employees is with production managers and directors in mining and energy (44 per cent) and assemblers of vehicles and metal goods (33 per cent); the lowest is in shopkeepers and wholesale and retail proprietors (negative 30 per cent), and merchandisers and window dressers (negative 28 per cent). Some of these jobs would in the past typically have been seen, of course, as 'male' or 'female' respectively.

Women are also more likely than men to leave their job because of a longer commute. Women still favour short commutes (15 minutes or fewer), while men do the majority of longer journeys to work (an hour or more). Again, this is tied to the fact that women are often the main providers of childcare and unpaid work, and therefore tend to favour the flexibility offered by a shorter commute. On the other hand, men are more likely to tolerate a longer journey to work in return for higher pay (and the chance to type very loudly on a laptop throughout the duration of a train trip, just in case anyone in the carriage hadn't clocked quite how intergalactically important they are).

The gender commuting gap follows exactly the same

Occupation	Hourly earnings (£)	Gender pay gap	Change from 2020
Managers, directors and senior officials	22.01	10.2	0.7
Professional occupations	22.06	9.2	2.9
Associate professional and technical occupations	16.44	10.9	2.2
Administrative and secretarial occupations	12.58	5.8	2.7
Skilled trades occupations	13.13	21.9	5.4
Caring, leisure and other service occupations	10.57	6.7	2.4
Sales and customer service occupations	10.66	2.9	4.8
Process, plant and machine operatives	11.67	16.1	5.0
Elementary occupations	10.26	11.0	5.2

Table 5: Gender pay gap for median gross hourly earnings (excluding overtime) for full-time employees by occupation group, year ending April 2021

age pattern as the gender pay gap. Both open up as people reach their mid- to late-20s, implying a link with having children (the average age of a first-time mother was 28.8 years in 2017). Women begin to sacrifice their longer commutes, bringing their average travel time down while average pay plateaus; but in the meantime men maintain their longer commutes while their pay continues to rise. Interestingly, given how much regional variation there is across so many statistics, these particular findings are largely the same regardless of where people live. If there is a hotspot for this trend, it's in the Guildford and Aldershot area, which spans part of Surrey and Hampshire: in other words, a commuter belt location outside London, to where couples move when starting a family, and with men more likely than women to continue working in the capital (in 2019, just before the pandemic disrupted traditional working patterns, the labour market in the City of London was more dependent than anywhere else in the country on commuters: it had 110.1 jobs for every inhabitant aged 16–64, followed by Westminster, with 4.2 jobs per inhabitant and Camden with 2.2). Of course, how much all this will change permanently as a result of the immediate shock to working patterns caused by the coronavirus pandemic, the resulting lockdowns and their effects on working life long-term is, still, anyone's guess.

THE EFFECTS OF TECHNOLOGY

Technology is, in general, a net benefit when it comes to productivity rates. Computers can do any number of tasks vastly quicker than humans. Smartphones, Wi-Fi, data transmission networks and videoconferencing have meant that workers are far less tied to the office (both physically and temporally) than they used to be. Some bank cashiers have been replaced by cash dispensers, factory workers have been replaced by machines, some supermarket cashiers by self-checkout machines,* and some delivery drivers by robots. As we've seen in the past, technology might change the nature of jobs but it doesn't necessarily remove the need for them completely. Think about the role of a secretary: 50 years ago this job was completely different than it is today, but the job still exists in some numbers (169,000 'personal assistants and other secretaries', according to the 2020 Annual Population Survey).

---

* On the other hand, this has led to a new job: The One Who Stands By The Self-Service Checkout And Shows People How To Use It. In some cases, this process is so slow and laborious that it takes way longer and uses more manpower than simply going back to the old cashier system would have done.

The extent to which current jobs are at risk from automation depends largely on the nature of that job. Lower-skilled jobs with repetitive tasks are more likely to be automated than are higher-skilled jobs, where human interaction is involved. It is not so much that robots are taking over, but that routine and repetitive tasks can be carried out more quickly and efficiently by an algorithm written by a human, or a machine designed for one specific function. The risk of automation tends to be higher for lower-skilled roles for this reason.

Taxi drivers are more at risk here than teachers or nurses, say: the latter two require emotional intelligence, empathetic thinking and the ability to adapt to different people's needs, whereas driving can be done by driverless cars (though in the interests of making the transition gradual, these cars may well be equipped with voice synthesisers pre-programmed with trenchant views on immigration, West Ham's transfer policy and the inadvisability of taking the A13 at rush hour).

A 2019 ONS study showed that around 1.5 million jobs in England – 7.4 per cent of the 20 million surveyed – were at high risk of some of their duties and tasks being automated in the future. The three occupations with the highest probability of automation were waiters and waitresses, shelf fillers and elementary sales occupations; the three least likely to be automated were medical practitioners, higher education teaching professionals, and 'senior professionals of educational establishments' (which is a fancy way of describing headteachers, college principals, school bursars and the like).

Women, young people and those who work part-time were most likely to work in roles that are at high risk of automation. More than two-thirds – 70.2 per cent – of the roles at high risk of automation were held by women. Of those aged 20 to 24 years who were employed, 15.7 per cent were in jobs at high risk of automation. The risk of job automation decreased for older workers, and was lowest for workers aged 35–39 years. Just 1.3 per cent of people in this age bracket were in roles at high risk of automation. The risk then increased again from the age group 40 to 44 upwards.

This pattern can be explained by the fact that workers naturally obtain further skills and become more knowledgeable in their field as they progress further in their careers. When young workers enter the labour market, they may be entering part-time roles and employed in industries such as sales, retail and other roles, where some degree of automation is highly likely. Many young workers may move through a range of roles before settling into a career. In addition, younger workers have more time and opportunity to retrain or change career paths.*

Technology has also made homeworking much easier, at least for employees in certain sectors where physical proximity to colleagues, suppliers and clients is not always of paramount importance. More than half of those in the information and communication industry reported having worked from home in 2019, compared with only 10 per cent in the accommodation and food services industry, and the extent to which companies in these sectors invested in ICT, software and hardware to enable homeworking reflects this: £9,196 per worker in information and communications,

---

* We can also partially explain the increase in the risk of automation from the age of 35 years with the change in working patterns, particularly for women. From the age of 30 years, more women work part-time, and this increases until women reach the age of 50 years, when it then steadily drops down. People who work part-time are more likely to work in roles at a higher risk of automation, but ultimately your occupation determines the probability of automation, not your working pattern.

compared with just £272 in accommodation and food services.*

The nature of the work itself aside, the ability of an industry to engage in homeworking arrangements is dependent on three categories of technological indicator: accessibility (whether employees can access the required technology remotely), usage (social media and information-sharing software can help here) and skills (the extent to which employees are trained in technological matters).

Twenty years ago, social media was more or less unknown, and even a decade ago it was in many respects a shadow of what it is now. These days, it's seen as a pretty essential part of many companies' brand and commercial image; more than two-thirds of

* These figures predate the coronavirus pandemic which obliged many more people than before to work from home (or perhaps to think of ever more creative ways in which watching Netflix could be construed as an essential work-related activity). During the period 9 April to 20 April 2020, for example, 45 per cent of adults in employment said they had worked from home at some point in the last week. This was while stringent lockdown measures were in force. By late October 2021 businesses reported that 61 per cent of their staff were working from their designated workplaces, though that proportion then fell back somewhat as the Omicron variant struck.

*Figure 17: People who work from home who use
both a telephone and computer to do so*
Source: Office for National Statistics

companies use it for this purpose and/or to market products, particularly in retail (87 per cent) and accommodation/food services (86 per cent). Within every

Figure 18: People who work from home using both a telephone and computer who need both to be able to work
Source: Office for National Statistics

industry, at least one-quarter of all businesses using social media use it to obtain or respond to customers' opinions.

TERMS AND CONDITIONS APPLY

In recent decades, the length of the working week hasn't generally changed very much: full-timers on average did 38.1 hours a week in 1993, and after some ups and downs, partly as a result of the state of the economy, by the end of 2019 it was 36.9 hours.*

However, this is much shorter than it used to be. In 1810, the standard daily hours of work for Glasgow bricklayers were seven in winter and 10 in summer – so, as that would have been six days a week, a summer week of 60 hours. By 1880 it had come down to 51 hours in summer and 43 in winter. In London, much further south, of course, brickies were expected to put in 47 hours a week in winter, but at least got 9d. an hour compared with the 7d. that was all the canny Glaswegian contractors were paying their men. By 1926, hours of work for London bricklayers had been standardised at 44 hours a week all year

---

* Of course, in early 2020 average hours plunged, as there were large numbers of people on furlough still counting as in employment but not actually doing any hours. Since then it has largely – but not entirely – gone back to where it was before the pandemic.

round, where it stayed for many years. More northerly cities kept the distinction between winter and summer hours much longer, but by 1968 a year-round week of just 40 hours seems to have been standard for bricklayers across the country. Men working in agriculture, meanwhile, were expected to do 58 hours a week in 1914, for a princely threepence-ha'penny an hour.

As we've already seen, work can be dangerous. In 1885, a total of 4,257 people were killed in industrial accidents, of which just over half related to shipping. With the economy expanding and the number of people in work growing, it is not surprising that the number of deaths was rising too – it peaked at 5,235 in 1912, the only year it went above 5,000. But perhaps that is partly because that year saw deaths in shipping accidents go back above 2,000 for the only time in the twentieth century, presumably partly because of the 685 crew members who went down with RMS *Titanic* that year. Meanwhile, it is perhaps not too surprising to find that the death toll from 'factory processes', which had been creeping up from 379 in 1885 to 996 in 1913, presumably as industry grew, suddenly tipped above the thousand mark in 1915 and peaked at 1,357 in 1918 (in which year 134 people were killed in a single moment when a munitions factory in Chilwell, Nottinghamshire, exploded). Deaths in shipping accidents were actually down during the First World War, though presumably those figures exclude people killed by enemy action. The total number of deaths, which as we saw was above 5,000 in 1912, dipped below a thousand for the first time in 1967, when 952 died. According to the Health and Safety Executive, just 142 people were killed at work in Great Britain in 2020–21, less than 3 per cent of the UK death toll in 1912. So next time you're told at work that you can't do something as seemingly harmless as hanging Christmas decorations from the office ceiling, give the health-and-safety people a break.

The late nineteenth and early twentieth centuries saw an upswell in labour discontent and strikes, which is presumably what led to the compilation of official statistics on the number of days lost to strikes, starting in 1891. Before the First World War, the peak year for going on strike was 1912, when 41 million working days were lost; but that was dwarfed by the 86 million days lost in 1921 in the immediate aftermath of the war. 1926 saw not only the General Strike but also a long-running miners' strike, and in all a staggering 162 million working days were lost

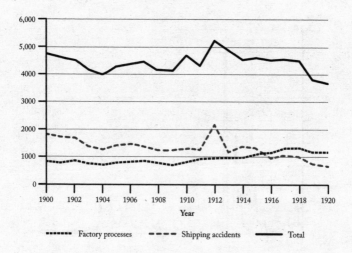

Figure: 19 Deaths at work 1900–1920
Source: Office for National Statistics

(146 million of them in coal mining) – and this total is still the all-time record. The post-war decades were much quieter – but by the 1970s the industrial truce was breaking down. Several years stand out – 1972, 1974, when a miners' strike brought the three-day week, 1979 which saw the 'winter of discontent' that ushered in the Thatcher years, and then 1984, which saw the start of another long-running miners' strike – which, along with the Falklands War, was arguably one of the two defining struggles of her premiership.

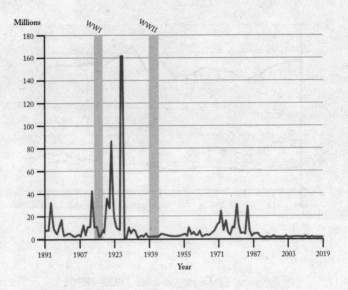

Figure 20: Working days lost to labour disputes, 1891–2019
Source: Office for National Statistics

Meanwhile, even the ways people are employed has been changing over time; although it fluctuates, generally speaking more of us are our own bosses. In 1959, around 7 per cent of jobs were filled by self-employed people; by 2019 that had almost doubled, to 13 per cent. But it isn't a straight line; there was something of a self-employment boom from the late 1970s and 1980s to the mid-1990s, when it peaked at over 12 per cent, before falling again around the turn of the millennium, only to revive thereafter. The number of self-employed people was particularly affected by the coronavirus pandemic, falling rapidly at the outset and to date not recovering. In the first quarter of 2020, the self-employed accounted for 15.1 per cent of all those in employment, but by the fourth quarter of 2021 this was just 12.8 per cent.

PART THREE

WHERE WE LIVE

A sense of place, where we come from and where we have settled in life, is a vital part of who we are as individuals. And as we shall see, there is a great deal of variety in the different places the people of the UK live, whether that is a large, densely populated city, a smaller town or a remote rural area. Likewise there is no standardisation in the type of dwellings we inhabit, whether a high-rise flat, a semi-detached house or even that most quintessentially British of suburban dwellings, the bungalow (though they actually account for less than 10 per cent of the housing stock in England), nor in the different types of tenure. But in all of this, as with the other topics we've looked at, official statistics give us a guide to how some of this has changed down the years.

TOWN AND COUNTRY

In 1801, fewer than a fifth of people lived in cities with more than 20,000 people; by 1891 that figure was more than half. Urbanisation has been an inevitable consequence of industrialisation the world over, and the UK has been no exception – indeed, as the cradle of the Industrial Revolution, it was among the first countries to experience this. Industrialisation not only draws people to the cities, but it enables the production of machinery, which in turn makes agrarian work easier and more efficient, which in turn means fewer jobs for farm workers, who have to come to the cities to seek alternative employment (the number of farmworkers fell from 2.017 million in 1851 to 1.496 million in 1911), and so on.

The census of 1831 showed that, by then, London had 1,471,410 inhabitants, which meant – even though, of course, the census-takers had no idea of this at the time – that it had probably just overtaken Beijing as the most populous city in the world, a status on to which it would hang for close on 100 years before ceding it to New York in the 1920s. London's population had increased by 20 per cent in the decade before

1831, and though it still dwarfed every other city in Britain, as it had for centuries, some of them were growing even faster than the capital was. Over that same period, Manchester (227,808) had grown 47 per cent, Glasgow (202,425) 44 per cent, Liverpool (189,202) 44 per cent and Birmingham (142,206) 33 per cent. In demographic terms, the 1820s had seen the full effect of the Industrial Revolution. Indeed, Manchester – then the centre of the global textile industry and nicknamed 'Cottonopolis' for its mills – was pretty much the world's first industrial city, and in the 80 years following 1831, grew by 1,000 per cent to 2.3 million. Bradford grew by 50 per cent every decade between 1811 and 1851, by which time only half its population had actually been born there.

This rapid rate of growth could not, and did not, come without its fair share of problems. In 1844, Friedrich Engels published *The Condition of the Working Class in England*, the most comprehensive record of living conditions in these newly industrialised cities. Engels described what were effectively shanty towns: people living cheek by jowl in shacks, sometimes with dirt floors and/or partially open to the elements, and in sanitary conditions so atrocious that disease could spread like wildfire. It wasn't unknown for mill workers to sleep eight, 10, even 12 to a room with no furniture or bedding; perhaps with a pile of straw or sawdust, which of course meant that they were treated no better than animals. Tuberculosis, cholera, smallpox, rickets, scarlet fever and typhoid were all common.

The same year, 1844, George Reynolds wrote of London that:

> the most unbounded wealth is the neighbour of the most hideous poverty. The crumbs which fall from the tables of the rich would appear delicious viands to starving millions, and yet these millions obtain them not! In that city there are in all five prominent buildings: the church, in which the pious pray; the gin-palace, to which the wretched poor resort to drown their sorrows; the pawn-broker's, where miserable creatures pledge their raiment, and their children's raiment, even unto the last rag, to obtain the means of purchasing food, and – alas! too often – intoxicating drink; the prison, where the victims of a vitiated condition of society expiate the crimes to which they have been drive by starvation and despair; and the workhouse, to which the destitute, the aged, and the friendless hasten to lay down their aching heads – and die!

Moral of the story: don't read Reynolds when you just want some good old-fashioned escapism.

By 1861, London's population had more or less doubled from its 1831 level to reach 2,803,989, and only three-fifths of its inhabitants had been born there. The influx came from all parts of the country: former farm labourers seeking more reliable and better-paid work in industry, women and girls sent to the city to seek a life in domestic service, and so on. 'The stream to London from the South grows larger,' noted Registrar General George Graham, 'and the counties of Cornwall, Devon, Somerset, Dorset and Wilts send 128,442 of their natives to be enumerated in London – 70 natives to every 1,000 of the inhabitants of these South-western counties.' Proportionally, however, East Anglia accounted for almost double that number, with 133 natives out of every 1,000 from Essex, Suffolk, Norfolk, Cambridgeshire and Lincolnshire combined making their way to streets paved, if not with gold, then at least with opportunity and dynamism. Half a century later, a government report would say, with a staggering lack of tact, 'all the best blood, young spirits with higher aspirations, leave for the towns or abroad. Only the old and children are left with the indifferent.' It was not all doom and gloom in terms of conditions in London, however: the mid-Victorian years saw not only the construction of Bazalgette's sewer system in London but also early public health legislation, starting with the Public Health Act 1872. In his report for 1881, the then registrar general wrote:

> *Let us then take the entire period of ten years that elapsed between the Public Health Act and the close of 1881. Had the death-rate remained during that period at its mean level in the preceding decade, the total deaths from 1872 to 1881 inclusively would have been 5,548,116; whereas they were actually no more than 5,155,367. Thus no less [sic] than 392,749 persons who under the old regime would have died were, as a matter of fact, still living at the close of 1881. Add to these lives saved the avoidance of at least four times as many attacks of non-fatal illness, and we have the total profits as yet received from our sanitary expenditure.*

Yet despite the general clean-up, conditions in the poorest parts of London continued to be pretty dire. Of the million inhabitants of the East End of London counted in the 1881 census, a third lived in poverty, and with that came stratospheric levels of crime and debauchery. When the American author Jack London came to, er, London in 1902, the famous travel agency Thomas Cook refused to provide him with a guide in the East End and advised him to ask the police instead. He eventually persuaded a cab driver to take him to Stepney, which he described as:

> *one unending slum. The streets were filled with a new and different race of people, short of stature, and of wretched or beer-sodden appearance. We rolled along through miles of bricks and squalor, and from each cross street and alley flashed long vistas of bricks and misery. Here and there lurched a drunken man or woman, and the air was obscene with sounds of jangling and squabbling.*

Noting that recruitment drives for the Boer War had shown that almost four in every five working-class Londoners were unfit for army service, London added of the slum dweller that:

> *the air he breathes, and from which he never escapes, is sufficient to weaken him mentally and physically, so that he becomes unable to compete with the fresh virile life from the country hastening on to London*

Town. It is incontrovertible that the children grow
up into rotten adults, without virility or stamina, a
weak-kneed, narrow-chested, listless breed, that
crumples up and goes down in the brute struggle for
life with the invading hordes from the country.

Indeed, this seems to have remained a problem thereafter, to judge by an account from the German-based American war correspondent William L. Shirer. He described the first British prisoners of war he saw in 1940 as having 'hollow chests, round shoulders, pasty complexions and bad teeth – tragic examples of the youth that England [*sic*] had neglected so irresponsibly in the years between the wars'.

And still, of course, London continued to grow: 5 million in 1901 and 7 million in 1911. However, its growth would later pause and indeed reverse for a while. By 1931 it had reached 8.1 million souls; but at 8.2 million it was barely any bigger by 1951 (this after, of course, the destruction wrought by the Blitz and the subsequent deliberate policy decision to encourage people to relocate outside London to the New Towns). The city's 1991 population of 6.8 million was a sixth down on where it had been 40 years before, though thereafter the capital's population has been growing again. By 2011, the influx of people to London from all corners of the globe rather than just all corners of the kingdom meant that, for the first time, 'white British' was not the majority resident profile. That London contained residents from almost every country in the world was not surprising; what was perhaps more surprising was that 39 nationalities could each boast at least 20,000 residents on the previous census day of 27 March 2011, a sizeable community in anybody's book (and indeed in this book too). Indians (262,247) and Poles (158,300) were top of the tree, and among the others were 129,807 Irish, 87,467 Jamaicans, 66,654 French, 63,920 Americans, 62,050 Italians, 55,476 Germans, 53,959 Australians, 30,880 Spaniards, 27,288 Canadians and 20,637 Japanese.

There had long been a distinctly Irish tinge to the influx into Manchester, a tinge which was even more pronounced following the potato famine of the 1840s. Around 35 per cent of today's population of Manchester and Salford is thought to have some kind of Irish ancestry. In addition, large numbers of central and eastern Europeans – mainly Jewish – came, and Manchester's 40,000-strong Jewish community today is the largest outside London. The pace of growth and change gave a real dynamism, even recklessness, to parts of civic life: not just new industrial processes but also political thought (the 'Manchester School' of economic and political thought promoted laissez-faire regulatory attitudes and free trade), radical religious sects and labour organisations, and so on. As a saying of the time went, 'what Manchester does today the rest of the world does tomorrow', and in his novel *Coningsby* (also published in 1844, which was clearly the year for such things), Benjamin Disraeli (at the time a back-bench MP and writer) wrote that, 'Manchester is as great a human exploit as Athens.'

At the beginning of the nineteenth century, Birmingham had a population of around 74,000. By 1851 this had more than trebled to 230,000, and by the end of the century it had further grown to 630,000, en route becoming the second largest city in the country. Like Manchester, it took in many Irish immigrants during and after the potato famine. Where Manchester had cotton, Birmingham had metalwork in all shapes and sizes, so much so that it became known as the 'City of a Thousand Trades': buttons, cutlery, guns, jewellery, locks, nails, ornaments, screws, tools, toys and many more were all made there. And until late in the century, its industry was still mainly centred around small workshops rather than large factories.

Birmingham was no more immune to housing problems than any other fast-growing city. More than 150,000 houses were built between 1919 and 1954, but even so, around a fifth were deemed unfit for human habitation, necessitating a massive programme of slum clearance and high-rise building. The post-war years also saw large-scale immigration from Commonwealth countries such as India, Pakistan, Bangladesh and various Caribbean islands, which in turn brought both vibrancy and racial tensions: it was no coincidence that Enoch Powell chose Birmingham in which to deliver his notorious 'Rivers of Blood' speech in 1968.

It was not just the big cities where population growth brought social problems in its wake. York, which in medieval times had been the second city of England, had only 17,000 inhabitants in 1801; but in the following decades it became an important centre for the growing railway network. It reached 40,000 people by 1851 and 75,000 by 1901. However, York also had a strong Quaker tradition, connected with the leading families in the confectionery trade, and this promoted an interest in social conditions and reform. In 1901, Seebohm Rowntree published his study on conditions in York, *Poverty, a Study of Town Life*; this showed that of the 46,000 people he surveyed, nearly two-fifths lived in poverty, which he defined as lacking the income 'necessary to enable families to secure the necessities of a healthy life'. Meanwhile, as early as 1864, the registrar general had noted the low mortality rates of some of the resort towns, and even predicted an early form of 'health tourism':

> *nearly all the English watering places are on good sites ... and there can be no doubt that ultimately England will be the resort of foreigners who are in search of health, when we find a mortality-rate per 1,000 so low as 15 in the Isle of Wight, 16 in Newton Abbot, including Torquay, 17 in Cheltenham, 17 in Eastbourne, 18 in Worthing, 18 in Barnstaple, including Ilfracombe, 18 in Mutford, including Lowestoft*

However, he then went to complain of other resorts being 'very unreasonable to throw into the waters where visitors bathe the offensive matters which would fertilize the disinfecting chalk soils in the surrounding fields'.

DON'T FENCE ME IN

The 2011 census showed that 95 per cent of the population lived in built-up areas, defined as land that is 'irreversibly urban in character'.* These don't have to be cities or towns: villages count too, with populations beginning at just over 100 (the two smallest being Broadwell in West Oxfordshire and Heapham in West Lindsey). In England, 1,502,015 hectares are classified as urban by the Ordnance Survey, with another 90,535 in Wales and 176,009 in Scotland. This works out at 11.3 per cent of the total area in England, 4.4 per cent in Wales and just 2.3 per cent in Scotland – or in total less than 8 per cent. So, yes, this is a crowded island, but equally 92 per cent of the land in Great Britain is not used for housing or otherwise urbanised at all, so there is still plenty of space for those who, like Greta Garbo, just want to be alone.

There are obvious and perhaps predictable correlations between the size of a settlement and the

---

* They include areas of built-up land with a minimum of 20 hectares. Any areas with less than 200 metres between them are linked to become a single built-up area.

characteristics of those who live there. The larger settlements are – that is, as villages give way to towns and towns to cities – the more likely the residents are to be younger, living in a socially rented home, born outside the UK and have no access to a private motor vehicle. They are less likely to be white and Christian. In 2011, three-fifths of residents in built-up areas were aged below 45, whereas 54 per cent of residents in non-built-up areas were aged 45 and over, reflecting among other things the concentration of universities in towns and cities and the tendency for people to retire to rural areas, especially, of course, the seaside. Indeed, so strong is the latter tendency that in mid-2020, of the 10 local authorities in Great Britain with the highest percentage of their populations aged 65 or over, all 10 were coastal areas.

The most common age groups for built-up areas in 2011 were 15 to 29 (20 per cent) and 30 to 44 (21 per cent), whereas the most common age groups for non-built-up areas were 45 to 59 (24 per cent) and 60 to 74 (21 per cent). The biggest difference between the two types of area was in the 60 to 74 age group, with built-up areas having 14 per cent of usual residents in this age group, compared with 21 per cent in non-built-up areas.

Great Britain, mid-2020	
North Norfolk	33.5
Rother	32.3
East Devon	30.5
East Lindsey	30.4
Tendring	29.9
New Forest	29.6
Dorset Unitary Authority	29.4
Arun	29.1
Isle of Wight	28.7
South Lakeland	28.7

Table 6: Percentage of population aged 65 or over –
the top ten local authorities
Source: Office for National Statistics

Four major built-up areas comprised those areas of more than a million people. They were Greater London (which by 2020 had reached 9.002 million residents), the West Midlands (2.940 million), Greater Manchester (2.848 million) and West Yorkshire (2.345 million). The seven large built-up areas were Bristol,

Category	Usual residents	Built-up areas	Resident population	%
Non built-up	–	–	2,703,100	4.8
Minor	<10,000	4,999	7,646,500	13.6
Small	10,000–99,999	424	11,826,500	21.1
Medium	100,000–499,999	59	12,303,900	21.9
Large	500,000–999,999	7	5,036,100	9.0
Major	1,000,000+	4	16,559,700	29.5

Table 7: Usually resident population in built-up and non-built-up areas of England and Wales, 2011
Source: Office for National Statistics

Leicester, Liverpool, Nottingham, Sheffield, South Hampshire and Tyneside.

Taking all this together, in 2020 the overall population over the UK was 67.1 million people. Being dispersed as they were over the 242,741 square kilometres of the country, that means that the population density of the UK as a whole was 276 people per square kilometre, but of course they weren't spread evenly. The highest population densities were, not surprisingly, to be found in London, topped by Tower Hamlets at over 16,000 people per square kilometre, and indeed all 20

0–150   151–300   301–450   451–600   600+

People per square kilometre

Figure 21: UK population density, mid-2020
Source: Office for National Statistics

	People per square kilometre
London	5,727
North West	522
South East	483
West Midlands	459
Yorkshire and the Humber	359
East	328
North East	312
East Midlands	311
South West	237
Wales	153
Northern Ireland	137
Scotland	70

Table 8: Population density, 2020
Source: Office for National Statistics

of the most densely populated local authorities are in the capital, before Portsmouth comes in at number 21 on the list. Likewise, with Scotland by far the least densely populated part of the UK (barely half the density of Northern Ireland, the next lowest), one might expect to see a number of the remoter parts of

Top five local authorities by density	
Tower Hamlets	16,791
Islington	16,699
Hackney	14,752
Kensington and Chelsea	12,939
Camden	12,834
Bottom five local authorities by density	
Orkney Islands	23
Shetland Islands	16
Argyll and Bute	12
Highland	9
Na h-Eileanan Siar	9

Table 9: Population densities, 2020
Source: Office for National Statistics

Scotland on the list of the least dense local authorities in the country – and indeed Na h-Eileanan Siar, which covers the Outer Hebrides, has fewer of us to the square kilometre than anywhere else.

Naturally, the growing population means that population density has also been increasing overall: for the UK as a whole, it went from 244 people in 2001 to, as

I said, 276 in 2020. But this hasn't been even across the whole country: the highest percentage growths in population density were in Tower Hamlets, the City and Newham, areas partly affected by the ongoing redevelopment of the Docklands.

A HOME OF ONE'S OWN?

Margaret Thatcher famously wanted to create a nation of homeowners. In her very first speech as leader of the Conservative Party in 1975, she spoke of a 'property-owning democracy', and she had only been prime minister for a year when, in 1980, she introduced the 'right to buy', which, by allowing council tenants to buy their properties at discounted prices, transformed the housing market.* But, whereas those who were in middle age during her administration have largely reaped the benefits of this policy – in 2020–21 almost three-quarters of people aged 65 years and over in England owned their home outright (up from 56 per

---

* The idea had reportedly been previously rejected by Labour Prime Minister Jim Callaghan. Thatcher saw it for what it was – something that chimed perfectly with the hopes and ambitions of the aspirational working classes whose votes she sought.

cent in 1993), having either originally bought with cash or paid off their mortgage over the years – the same doesn't hold true for the generations that have followed Thatcher's children.

Younger people are less likely to own their own home than in the past and more likely to be renting. Over half of people in their mid-30s to mid-40s had a mortgage in 2020–21, compared with two-thirds in 1997. Almost two-fifths of people in this age bracket now rent their homes, and in 2020–21 a quarter were renting from a private landlord, compared with fewer

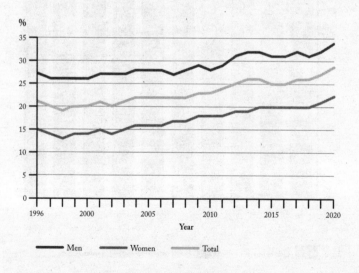

Figure 22: Young people aged 20–34 living with their parents
Source: Office for National Statistics

than 1 in 10 in 1997. These changes were particularly pronounced in the decade between 2001 and 2011, when the proportion of owner-occupied homes decreased from 69 per cent to 64 per cent – the first fall in a century. Another trend, of course, is for young people to remain living with their parents for longer than in previous generations. ONS figures show that, in 1996, barely a fifth of people aged between 20 and

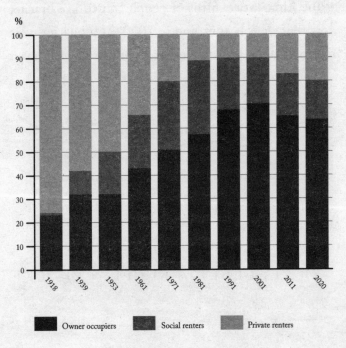

Figure 23: 100 years of tenure
Source: Department for Levelling Up, Housing and Communities

34 lived with their parents; by 2020 this had risen to almost three-tenths in total, and over a third for the men. The UK is not alone among European countries in having its young men often remaining at home; indeed, the Italians have a word, *mammoni*, to describe young men still living under their mothers' roofs.

Though rising, the proportion of renters is still way down on what it was a hundred years ago. At the end of the First World War, more than three-quarters of the population were tenants, almost all of them renting from private landlords, as social housing was still very much in its infancy.

HOUSE PRICES

Ah, house prices. The ONS doesn't offer an official league table of our national obsessions, but if it did, then house prices would surely be duking it out for a position on the podium with the weather and, for the younger among us at least, what happened on last night's *Love Island*.

To our eyes, houses of the past seem absurdly cheap. The 1910 land tax valuations reveal that even grand London houses went, in cash terms, for no more than the price of a family saloon these days: you could have bought a house in Chancery Lane for £11,000, one in Cannon Street for £20,000 and one in Fleet Street for £25,000 (or £150, even today, if you're buying that property on the Monopoly board). The valuations also pegged the Bank of England at £110,000 and the Mansion House opposite it at £992,000. (St Paul's Cathedral was classed as exempt.)*

Before the Second World War, most new houses sold for less than £750. In 1926, for example, when the Queen was born, the average house cost £619; by the 1950s the average house price was £1,891, though equally the average worker took home only around £520 per annum. By the 1960s houses were £2,530,

---

* These valuations followed Chancellor David Lloyd George's 'People's Budget' of the previous year, in which he had pledged to tax the rich through their properties: 'we sent the hat round amongst the workmen and winders of Derbyshire and Yorkshire, the weavers of the High Peak and the Scotsmen of Dumfries, who all dropped in their coppers,' he said in Limehouse, one of the poorest areas in London, on 30 July 1909. 'We went round Belgravia and there has been such a howl ever since that it has completely deafened us. No country, however rich, can permanently afford to have quartered upon its revenue a class which declines to do the duty which it was called upon to perform. I say their day of reckoning is at hand.' The rich, predictably, were up in arms. One duke threatened to set his hounds on Lloyd George.

earnings £960 and high-rise blocks – 'streets in the sky' – were revolutionising the housing landscape. Virtually all houses had electricity by now, and most people had a refrigerator, cooker and TV too (TV ownership went from 25 per cent at the start of the decade to more than 80 per cent by the end). The 1970s saw a huge change in the housing market, with average prices going from £3,920 in January 1970 to £19,273 in January 1980 as mortgages became ever more widely available. The less said about seventies interior décor the better, however.* And the eighties increased the pace of change yet more. In January 1985, the average home cost £27,823; by the beginning of 1990, it was £58,250.

And prices have continued to rise, with only the occasional interludes of falling prices: in November 2021, the average dwelling cost £271,000, a far cry from the £3,757 it had been in 1969. In the two decades between 1995 and 2015, the number of houses sold for £1 million or more in England and Wales increased more than 70-fold. In 2015, 13,679 houses – that is, 1.6 per cent of all residential properties sold – were sold for £1 million or more. But in the

---

* For the real masochists among you, the video for 'Our House' by Madness gives the general idea.

prosperous borough of Kensington and Chelsea, 57 per cent of all properties sold that year went for seven figures – the first time in history that a majority of houses in a given area had ever sold at that level. Westminster had the second highest proportion of sales of £1 million or more properties, at 42 per cent.

One measure of house prices is their relationship to wages. In 2020, the ratio of median house prices to annual earnings was 7.84 in England and Wales as a whole, with an average house price of £249,000 and average earnings of £31,766. Not surprisingly, this

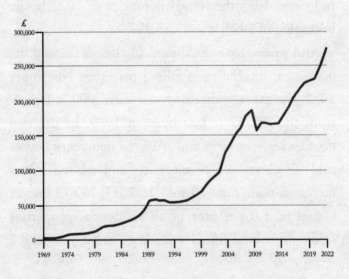

Figure 24: UK average house prices, 1969–2022
Source: Office for National Statistics and HM Land Registry

varied greatly across the country, with the most affordable region being the North East, where in 2020 house prices were only about five times annual earnings, compared with London, where that ratio was about 12½ times. Moreover, after a period where house prices became more affordable generally in the wake of the 2008 downturn, the 'affordability gap', if one might call it that, opened up faster in London than in the country as a whole.

Those who study these things have suggested that the current ratio between house prices and earnings is more or less as high as any point in the previous 100

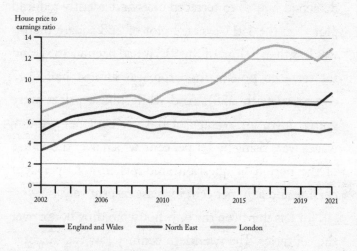

Figure 25: Housing affordability, 2002–2021
Source: Office for National Statistics

years but nowhere near the heights reached in the nineteenth century. In 1845, for example, house prices were running at 13 times the level of wages, but then fell more or less consistently for three-quarters of a century before bottoming out after the First World War. Why the fall? There were three main reasons: more houses, smaller houses and rising wages. In the six decades between 1851 and 1911, the Victorians and Edwardians more than doubled the housing stock, from 3.8 million houses to 8.9 million houses: towns and cities increasing in size, and transport improvements allowing the development of suburbs. With this came a shift from detached houses to terraced ones and a vastly reduced plot size: the 1911 average plot of 268 square metres was less than a third of the 913 it had been in 1851, and for terraced houses the drop was almost half (147 compared with 278). And while house prices were going down an average of 0.4 per cent per annum, wages were rising by 1.1 per cent, which over the course of the period in question amounts to a 23 per cent decline and a 90 per cent increase respectively.

Nor has this been the only housebuilding boom over the centuries. The twentieth century saw two massive spikes: a private sector boom after the First World War, going from more or less zero new houses in 1916 to more than 350,000 in 1936, and a public sector boom following the Second World War, up again from minimal levels in 1946 to around 425,000 two decades later. This was, of course, a matter of national importance, not to say emergency: half a million homes had been destroyed by German bombing during the war, and some of the first prefabs put up after the war were built in just 40 man-hours (often by prisoners of war). Indeed, between April and December 1945, local authorities had already built 8,939 temporary houses in England and Wales and another 437 in Scotland. Not that the construction industry had been idle during the war either, but of the total of £470 million worth of construction carried out in Great Britain in 1941 alone, no less than £120 million went into airfields and army depots; £76 million into new factories and warehouses; £63 million into repairs and clearance following air raids; £42 million into air-raid shelters; and only £22 million into the construction of houses and hostels.* The post-war decades were also a

* The Central Statistical Office, one of the organisations that was merged to form the ONS in 1996, was itself set up during the war at the behest of Winston Churchill, who had found that 'the utmost confusion is caused when people argue on different statistical data' and wanted government statistics combined into a central branch.

boom time for slum clearances: an average of 67,000 homes a year were demolished or closed down between 1955 and 1980, peaking at 95,000 in 1971.

Since the end of the Second World War, there has been a considerable shift in who is providing new housing. Generally, it was local authorities that led the post-war boom in new housing, being responsible for over four-fifths of completions in every year between 1948 to 1952. Thereafter the private sector picked up, going from barely 25,000 completions in 1950 to over 150,000 in 1960. The number of local authority completions tailed off dramatically in the 1980s, going from almost 75,000 in 1980 to less than 15,000 in 1990. Virtually all social housing is now built by housing associations, which were responsible for less than 1 per cent of all new houses just after the war, but which now provide about a sixth of new homes.

As to whether our society could see a fall in house prices relative to earnings similar to that witnessed by the Victorians and Edwardians – well, don't hold your breath. There are already 28 million homes in the UK, and it's hard to see how that could be doubled even if

---

In 1995 it published *Fighting with Figures: a Statistical Digest of the Second World War*, from which these construction figures come.

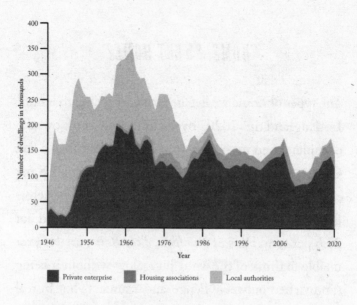

Figure 26: House building in England by tenure, 1946–2020
Source: Department for Levelling Up, Housing and Communities

every new home was sized for hobbits rather than humans. In addition, many homeowners are heavily mortgaged and would struggle hugely if prices were to fall and reduce their loan-to-value cushion and/or push them into negative equity. However, much of the rise in average house prices relative to incomes between 1985 and 2018 is down to the decline in real interest rates, and a rise in these rates could have dramatic consequences for the housing market.

HOME, SWEET HOME?

The types of home we live in varies according to tenure. In England in 2020, over nine-tenths of owner-occupiers lived in some type of house rather than a flat. Of these houses, 'small terraced' accounted for 7.5 per cent, 'medium or large terraced' for 18.8 per cent, semi-detacheds for 29.3 per cent and detached houses for 25.6 per cent. Fans of *Rumpole of the Bailey* are for ever unable to think of the word 'bungalow' without it being sandwiched between 'Penge' and 'murders', but in real life this most quintessential of English dwellings (a style and a word brought back, like so much else, from British India) accounted for 7.7 per cent of owner-occupied dwellings. However, those who rent are much more likely to live in a flat than are the owner-occupiers: 45.4 per cent of private renters, 49.2 per cent of council tenants and 43.0 per cent of housing association tenants were in flats. Although we might think of the post-war tower block as the archetypal form of council flat, in fact only 8.5 per cent of council tenants lived in high-rise flats, compared with 38.8 per cent in low-rise flats and 1.9 per cent in converted flats, while a clear majority (50.8 per cent) lived in houses of one sort or another.

HOMELESSNESS

Homelessness is a perennial problem for any government, and one perhaps thrown into even sharper relief than usual by the coronavirus pandemic, which, temporarily at least, saw many rough sleepers housed in empty hotel rooms. You are most likely to be homeless if you are a single childless man aged between 25 and 49. Those younger than that are a little less likely to be homeless than they were; those over 60, however, are more likely to find themselves homeless than in the past.

The bare statistics mask the very real human cost not just of being homeless but also of the circumstances that have brought people to that point: issues of mental and physical health, financial difficulties, relationship breakdowns and vulnerability to crime. In the 2017–18 financial year, around a quarter of homeless applicants cited relatives or friends no longer willing or able to offer accommodation as the reason for loss of home, around a tenth blamed the non-violent breakdown of their relationship with a partner and just over another tenth reported a violent relationship breakdown. In recent years, more effort has gone into producing official statistics about homeless people, and in 2018, as part of this, the ONS began producing estimates of deaths among them, for England and Wales. This showed that in 2018 their mean age at death was 45 for men and 43 for women, compared with 76 and 81 respectively for the general population of England and Wales. Sadly, it turns out that two in five deaths of homeless people were related to drug poisoning.

There are, in general, two categories of homelessness: temporary accommodation and rough sleeping. When it comes to households in temporary accommodation,* England saw an 89 per cent increase between 2012 and 2021, up from 50,430 to 95,290; there was a sharp rise in the number of single-person households in temporary accommodation in 2020 as a result of the pandemic, while the number of households with children has been roughly stable for a few years.

The number of rough sleepers is by its nature harder to quantify. Best estimates for England suggest that the number almost doubled between 2013 and 2017, from 2,414 to 4,751. Thereafter it fell a little in 2018

---

* Across the UK, there is a large range in the type of temporary accommodation, including public sector and local authority or housing association stock; private sector accommodation, either leased or nightly paid; and alternative forms of accommodation, such as hostels, refuges, and bed-and-breakfast-style accommodation.

and 2019, with a much bigger drop to 2,688 in 2020 in the wake of the pandemic. By late 2021 it had fallen to 2,440. The figures for Wales (132 in October 2021) and Northern Ireland (18 in November 2020) were much smaller, while Scotland does not hold a formal census of rough sleepers to give these snapshots. Major cities, unsurprisingly, account for a large proportion of rough sleepers: London just over a quarter of England's, Cardiff about a fifth of Wales's and Belfast half of Northern Ireland's much smaller number.

BLUE PLAQUES

Blue plaques are placed on the sides of London buildings where notable people once lived. The majority are famous artists, politicians, scientists and writers, but some are more obscure and quirkier, such as anarchism theorist Prince Peter Kropotkin, Anna Maria Garthwaite (designer of Spitalfields silks), theatrical wigmaker Willy Clarkson, Mary Hughes (listed as 'friend of all in need') and, perhaps best of all, namer of clouds Luke Howard. This makes him sound a little like Fotherington-Thomas in the Molesworth books – 'hello clouds, hello sky' – but in fact Howard was both a successful manufacturing chemist and a founding member of the Askesian Society, a philosophical group to whom he presented his paper 'On the Modification of Clouds' in 1803. This paper set out the height and nature of clouds, and suggested classification names – cirrus, stratus, cumulus and nimbus – that are still used today.

The oldest surviving blue plaque is that awarded in 1867 to Napoleon III of France on King Street, St James's. It's the only one to be installed in the subject's lifetime: these days they have to have been dead for 20 years, by which time – or so the thinking goes – anything bad and hitherto hidden will have come out (such as with, for example, Jimmy Savile).

The current rule is also only one plaque per person, though before this was introduced there were many cases of multiple plaques: Lord Palmerston, William Gladstone and William Makepeace Thackeray have three each (the latter perhaps appropriate for the man who wrote *Vanity Fair*). Nor are multiple plaques confined to people. There are currently 19 cases of houses containing two plaques, including 20 Maresfield Gardens in Hampstead (Sigmund Freud and Anna Freud), 48 Paultons Square in Chelsea (Samuel Beckett, and physicist and Jutland veteran Patrick

Blackett, best known for his work in detecting U-boats during the Second World War and also for research into cosmic rays) and 29 Fitzroy Square in Fitzrovia (George Bernard Shaw and Virginia Woolf). The American poet Sylvia Plath has a plaque in Chalcot Square, Primrose Hill, but she also lived in nearby Fitzroy Road at number 23, which bore a plaque to her fellow poet, the Irishman W.B. Yeats.

More unusual is a pair of plaques on neighbouring houses – in fact, there's only one such instance, and rather splendidly it juxtaposes Jimi Hendrix and George Frideric Handel on Brook Street, Mayfair. Two extraordinary musicians, separated by one wall and two centuries! The house where Handel lived is where he wrote *Messiah* and *Zadok the Priest* (which has been used at every coronation since 1727), though Hendrix, when asked what he thought about living next to Handel, reportedly replied, 'To tell you the truth, I haven't heard much of the fella's stuff.'

There are also unofficial plaques, which often bear the wording 'placed by public subscription' or similar. One of these can be found in Garratt Lane, Tooting, to Sidney Lewis, who joined the army aged 12 in 1915, fought on the Somme for six weeks in 1916, and was only sent home when his mother sent a copy of his birth certificate to the War Office and demanded his return. He served in the Second World War (this time clearly of proper age) as a bomb disposal expert before running a pub in East Sussex. In Southwark, the council adopted a scheme for plaques voted for by local residents, and one went to Sam King, a passenger on the *Empire Windrush* and later the first black mayor of the borough. Another marks the birthplace of Phyllis Pearsall, inventor of the London *A–Z*.

The plaque on Hammersmith Terrace, Chiswick, to master calligrapher Edward Johnston may at first glance appear the same as usual, but look closer. It's in a different font from normal: in fact, it's in one which Johnston himself created, which is named after him, and which is still used across all Transport for London's branding and signage. There are three other plaques in this font, all of them to men associated with London Transport: Harry Beck (designer of the iconic Tube map), Frank Pick (who designed much of the Underground system) and Lord Albert Stanley Ashfield (London Transport's first chairman).

THANKFUL VILLAGES

'Thankful Villages' are villages that lost no men in the First World War, because all those who left to serve came home again. The term was popularised by the writer Arthur Mee in his 1936 book *Enchanted Land*, and after the Second World War the term 'doubly thankful' was coined to describe a village that had lost no soldiers in either war. Of the estimated 16,000 villages in the country, only 53 are thought to be thankful and just 17 doubly thankful. Five of the doubly thankful ones are:

- Catwick, Yorkshire. Village blacksmith John Hugill nailed a horseshoe and 30 coins to his forge doorpost during the First World War to represent the 30 men from the village who'd gone to fight. He cut a notch in one of the coins to represent the arm which Joseph Grantham left behind on one of the battlefields. The same tradition of horseshoe and coins was repeated during the Second World War because it had worked first time round, and again everyone who went also came back.

- Helperthorpe, Yorkshire, has a plaque in the church commemorating not just the 18 men who went and returned from the First World War, but also marking those who were gassed (George Cooper and Henry Whitehead), gassed and wounded (Percy Garrod) and captured (Charles Beavis).

- Hunstanworth, Durham. This village saw five of its young men fight in the First World War: a young man called Arthur Taylor and four of Edward and Anne Jameson's sons, Makepeace, Michael, Ted and Joshua. Makepeace was wounded twice in 1916 and later hospitalised by the Spanish flu pandemic in 1918; Joshua, only 16 at the start of the war, was hit in the leg by shrapnel, which stayed there for the rest of his life. On their return from war, all five soldiers were given a framed certificate wishing them 'a long and happy future'.

- Knowlton, Kent, has a 17-foot commemorative cross erected in 1919 after the local paper, the *Weekly Dispatch*, ran a competition to find the 'Bravest Village in the United Kingdom'; that was, the one with the largest proportion of men volunteering to serve in the armed forces before March 1915. Almost 400 villages competed, and Knowlton was declared the winner with just over 31 per cent (12 out of 39, of whom all obviously came back).

- Upper Slaughter, Gloucestershire. An apparent middle finger to nominative determinism here, though actually the name 'slaughter' in this context comes from the Saxon 'slohtre' – 'muddy place' – rather than anything to do with death or massacres. The 25 villagers who went and came back from the First World War included one woman, Agnes Witts, who served with the Voluntary Aid Detachment providing nursing care to soldiers.

Interestingly, gratitude was not a universal emotion in the thankful villages, at least not initially. Where almost every other village nearby was mourning the loss of some of their residents, young men who would otherwise have had long and full lives ahead of them, those villages where everyone had survived often felt shame and guilt, as though they had somehow not played their part or paid their price. Many villages therefore felt it quite wrong to celebrate this as some kind of triumph. And of course the fact that everyone came back alive did not mean that they were unaffected by what they'd been through – quite the opposite. The physical scars were obvious, the mental ones less so but in many ways more damaging.

PART FOUR

1921:
A CENSUS OF
ENLIGHTENMENT

Various things in the history one learns at school belong firmly in the past, or so we like to think. Along with Viking raids and witch trials, surely worldwide outbreaks of pestilence belong firmly in a history textbook? In fact, some of these things aren't quite as distant as we'd like to think – the last conviction under the Witchcraft Act dates back only to 1944, for a medium who divulged a military secret she claimed she'd heard from beyond the grave. And, just as the great Spanish flu outbreak of 1918–19 was almost slipping beyond living memory, the world was plunged into a new pandemic – coronavirus or COVID-19 – with severe effects that cannot yet be fully known. The last word on the pandemic and its demographic and economic effects won't be written for many years, as researchers continue to plough through the mass of data that is already accumulating. However, we can say that the 2021 census was the first to take place after the onset of the coronavirus pandemic and the implications for its findings, once these are published, will be vast: not simply in terms of death rates but also living arrangements, employment patterns and much more.

Historically, pandemics have been agents of great change, though this change has taken many forms. Sometimes pandemics have seen societies regress and become more reactionary and insular: in 1349, the city of Strasbourg blamed the Jews for the Black Death and killed all those who refused to convert to Christianity. Sometimes entire civilisations have been wiped out: smallpox succeeded where Hernán Cortés had failed in bringing the Aztecs to their knees in 1520. And sometimes giant leaps forward in medicine and science have resulted, such as John Snow's discovery in 1854 that cholera was carried in water rather than by air.

It is still too early to say with certainty what kind of long-term change COVID-19 will bring, for the lessons of one pandemic cannot necessarily be applied to the next. As the old adage goes: 'Once you've seen one pandemic, you've seen one pandemic.' But change there will be, for no society comes through an event like this unscathed; and the effects of that change will be seen in data and figures many years and decades from now.

A BATTLE ON TWO FRONTS

The 1921 census* came on the back not just of its own pandemic, the Spanish flu of 1918–19, but also, of course, the First World War. There has never been a time before or since when the character of the nation's demographics changed so dramatically from one census to the next. The census was not without other difficulties – because of industrial action, it had to be delayed to 19 June from the original date of 24 April, by which time all the schedules had been printed and distributed. An amendment slip was therefore produced, showing the revised date. To help defray the

---

* Incidentally, 1921 was the one and only time that the census date was changed, so far at least, given that the next census in Scotland has been delayed until 2022. This census was also the first one conducted under the 1920 Census Act, which contains a statutory prohibition on disclosure (and which is still in force). The 1921 census returns were published in 2022 under the government's non-statutory 100-year rule, which has itself been in place for census records since 1962, when the 1861 census was published. Since the 1931 census returns were destroyed by fire and there was no census in 1941 because of the Second World War, the 1921 forms, almost by accident, represent a snapshot that would remain in place for 30 years of immense social change.

cost of this, advertising appeared on the back of the amendment slip. Unfortunately the advertiser was the *Sunday Illustrated*, a new press venture of the swindler Horatio Bottomley MP, who shortly afterwards was exposed and spent five years in prison for fraud. No advertising has been allowed on census material since.

The registrar general at the time was the splendidly monikered Sylvanus Percival Vivian, and he began his preliminary report by saying:

The great events of the decennium thus concluded cannot fail to impress a character of uncommon significance upon the results of this Census, whether regarded as vestigial records of the passage of the War itself or as a source of enlightenment upon the many problems which the War has bequeathed to us. For such enlightenment, at the very time when it is most sorely needed, the country has been unusually at a loss, since there are but few questions today upon which guidance can be sought of the last Census across the great gulf of War which lies between. It is thus with a full sense of the heavy and responsible burden of service which this Census will be called upon to render that the operations now completed have been planned and carried out.

Around 700,000 British men had been killed during the war,* which helped contribute to the smallest decennial increase since the decade between the first two censuses in 1801 and 1811. (That was in absolute terms, of course; as a proportion of the total population, 1911–21 was far more egregious than 1801–11, and indeed than any other decade too.) The increase between 1911 and 1921 was 1.94 million, representing 5 per cent of the population, as compared with a 3.79 million (11 per cent) rise for the previous period between 1901 and 1911. It was the first time since 1841 that the population had risen by less than 2 million. Indeed, only two towns in the entire nation saw their populations increase by more than 5 per cent between 1911 and 1921, and even this figure was misleading: for the towns in question were the seaside resorts of Blackpool and Southend-on-Sea, and since the census had been delayed from its usual spring slot to one in mid-June, these resorts were consequently teeming with holidaymakers.

This mass slaughter of men in the prime of their lives had profound and traumatic consequences; and

---

* This is a complicated figure – the higher total usually cited from the Commonwealth War Graves Commission, of around 888,000, includes men from the colonies (but not places such as Canada, Australia or New Zealand, which had Dominion status).

the statistics, though horrific, barely hint at the human cost. By 1921 there were 1.6 million widows and 731,000 children without a father. As Vivian wrote:

> *The most striking feature of these proportions is the large excess of fatherless as compared with motherless children, the former outnumbering the latter in a ratio of nearly 3 to 1. Male mortality is markedly higher than the corresponding female mortality at all adult ages, and to this, aggravated in general by the higher average age of the fathers and in respect of this particular experience by the loss of men during the war, part of the excess must be due.*

It wasn't just death rates that had increased: birth rates had also fallen dramatically. The average number of births between 1901 and 1911 was 1.087 million per annum, but by 1918 only 787,000 were recorded, a drop of almost a third. The most obvious cause of this decline was of course the fact that so many men were away fighting in the trenches, but there was also a less tangible reason too: anecdotal evidence shows that many women felt uneasy at bringing children into a wartime world so unstable and dangerous. (It was no coincidence that 1920, by which time both the war and pandemic were over, saw a record 1.127 million babies born.) Either way, by 1921 females outnumbered males by 1.7 million (19.8 million women and girls, 18.1 million men and boys; for a total of 37.9 million), though again this doesn't tell the full story: even in normal times the numbers of men away on census night (serving in the armed forces, fishermen out at sea) meant that every census since the first in 1801 had recorded more women than men.

And at the end of the war came the flu. As the children's playground rhyme went:

> *I had a little bird*
> *Its name was Enza*
> *I opened the window*
> *And in-flu-enza.*

It was called the 'Spanish flu' as the first reported cases came from Spain (including that of King Alfonso XIII himself), though this was only because most of the belligerent countries in the war (including Britain) had newspaper blackouts on any stories which might negatively affect morale.* In the UK, as in other European

---

* Just as the Spanish version of *Fawlty Towers* saw Manuel come

countries, the virus was spread by soldiers returning home from the cramped and highly infectious trenches in northern France, first into the cities (the very first place to record a case was Glasgow) and then into the countryside. Symptoms included sore throats, headaches and loss of appetite, though in many cases recovery was swift; at least initially, doctors referred to it as 'three-day fever'.

For the unlucky ones, however, it was a different story. Symptoms could go from mild to fatal in less than 24 hours. In July 1918 a Leicester woman collapsed and died while talking to a doctor in the street. The brother of William Hall from Rosley, Cumbria, wrote in his diary that 'we did not know he ailed anything until the morning of the day he died'. Skin could turn bluey-violet in colour – 'heliotrope cyanosis', so named after the flower – when sufferers' blood oxygen fell to critical levels. Professor Roy Grist, a Glasgow physician, wrote:

---

from Italy rather than Barcelona, so the Spanish themselves called the flu the 'Naples soldier'. The German army called it 'Blitzkatarrh', and British troops referred to it as 'Flanders grippe' or the 'Spanish lady'. All rather reminiscent of attitudes in sixteenth-century England, where syphilis was the 'French pox'.

*it starts with what appears to be an ordinary attack
of* la grippe. *When brought to the hospital,
[patients] very rapidly develop the most vicious type
of pneumonia that has ever been seen. Two hours
after admission, they have mahogany spots over the
cheek bones, and a few hours later you can begin to
see the cyanosis extending from their ears and
spreading all over the face. It is only a matter of a
few hours then until death comes and it is simply a
struggle for air until they suffocate. It is horrible.*

The flu came in three waves: mild in spring 1918,
devastating in autumn 1918 and moderate in early
1919. More than half the country's doctors were at the
war front during the first two waves in 1918, and those
left behind were often run off their feet: a Kingston-
upon-Thames practitioner said 'from early morning till
late at night I have done nothing but rush from one flu
patient to another'. Shortages of undertakers and
gravediggers meant that many bodies lay unburied for
days. The registrar general concluded that the outbreak
had been responsible for about 184,000 civilian deaths
in Britain (84,000 males and 100,000 females), plus
about 14,000 men in military service. Globally, more
people in total died than had in the four years of the

Black Death in the fourteenth century (though of course the world's population had been much bigger in 1918 than in 1347–51), and only a few places in the world – the island of Marajo in Brazil's Amazon delta, St Helena in the South Atlantic and a handful of South Pacific islands – reported no cases at all. In contrast, by the end of February 2022 (by which time the COVID-19 pandemic was by no means over, of course), it was reckoned that total COVID-19 cases worldwide had reached 440 million, and deaths had almost reached million.

'DOCTORS WERE POWERLESS ...'

The social implications were most profound for young women – and particularly for middle-class young women, since a higher proportion of officers had been killed than those in lower ranks. Of those aged 25 to 34 in 1921, 1.158 million were unmarried women and 919,000 unmarried men: a gap of 239,000. Around half of these women would still be unmarried by the time of the 1931 census, and though this did not mean that they would all be left 'on the shelf' – women marrying into their forties was not uncommon in the

1930s – it did of course have a bearing on fertility rates, since childbirth out of wedlock was much less common than it is now and the medical advances that now help women conceive later in life were not yet available.

The disruption wasn't just confined to the domestic sphere either. For women who wanted to work, the war had been a godsend. It wasn't just that there had been more jobs around – 6.2 million at the peak, up from 4.9 million in peacetime – but that those jobs had to a large extent been better paid, more challenging and more rewarding than the ones previously available. Come 1918, however, 750,000 women were made redundant, their jobs either discontinued or handed over to demobilised troops. Indeed, it was the end of the war that more or less formalised marriage bars in nursing, teaching, the civil service and some private companies too, despite the 1919 Sex Disqualification (Removal) Act, which was meant to prevent discrimination because of sex or marriage within public offices and professions. A single statistic demonstrates the effect of this more than a photograph, or the thousands words that it's proverbially worth, could ever do: that the number of women in work, as a percentage of all women, was lower in 1921 than it had been in 1911.

Contemporary accounts of the 1918–19 pandemic show how similar public reactions were in some ways between Spanish flu and COVID-19. 'Doctors were powerless,' said John Pears Jackson of Keswick in Cumbria, who was 11 when the flu first hit. 'Strong men and women were dead in the course of a few days. People drank whisky and dosed themselves with all kinds of medicines. One farmer I knew swore he cured himself with paraffin oil.' Many schools were closed. Margaret Pitt, then a pupil at Gravesend's Milton Mount College, said that the school:

tried to get us all home early before the Easter holidays. Telegrams were sent to our parents. Our trunks were packed and sent off. Then we all came down to the main hall ready for our journey, in coats, hats and gloves, and our hand luggage. The nurse and her assistant were there with thermometers to see if we were developing the virus. I think about half of us were sent back to bed, some were very upset as they were anxious to go home. I was one of those who had to go to bed. We were given plenty of drink ... milk.

(Cheltenham College decided to do things in reverse and locked staff and pupils inside the building.) Thousands of workers in Belfast were laid up, affecting the operation of the city's famous shipyards, and the *Irish News* reported that pharmacists were being 'literally besieged'. Even prime ministers were not immune, either then or now. David Lloyd George spent ten days confined to a Manchester sickbed with a respirator to aid his breathing and the government keen to downplay the severity of his condition. Sounds familiar?

Then, as now, there was lots of advice, some of it useful and some less so. The *Western Daily Press* said:

> *Keep the mouth shut as much possible, avoid indigestion, go into the open air, be cheerful, don't go into crowds, avoid over-fatigue, eat vegetables and fruit (if they can be got), smoke little, as smoking has a tendency to lower the nervous power and the resistance of the nose, mouth, and throat to infection.*

The *Bexhill-on-Sea Observer* advised readers to catch later trains home, sit on the outside of buses* where

---

* The top deck of a double-decker was typically still open to the elements at this time, of course.

possible and wear an extra coat. Formalin was sprinkled on the floor of Brighton's public library and post office every morning, and a pamphlet recommended that people 'give up shaking hands for the present and give up kissing for all time'.* In London, the borough of Hackney recommended that victims stay isolated, go to bed the moment symptoms appeared, and gargle with potash and salt.

The main difference between Spanish flu and COVID-19, or more precisely the main difference in its effects (as the viruses themselves are not especially biologically similar), is in those most at risk. Spanish flu affected young adults most of all, particularly those between 20 and 30 years of age, and those aged 75 and above had the lowest death rate of all. COVID-19 is the exact reverse: the median age of those dying from it is 80 for men and 84 for women. To take just two stories from hundreds of thousands: Gunner Ivor John Hiley survived three years of war and barely a month of peace, dying of flu aged 32 nine days before Christmas 1918; and Captain William Leefe Robinson, awarded

---

* It is perhaps a measure of how far Brighton has come in the last century that it is now literally the last place in the country where you can imagine such a pamphlet being distributed.

the VC for being the first British pilot to shoot down a German airship* over Britain before becoming a prisoner of war after himself being shot down in France, was repatriated at the end of the war, only to succumb to the flu on 31 December 1918, aged just 23.

And for all the criticisms levelled at the government for their handling of the crisis, they have by any metric been better prepared and quicker to react than their predecessors were in 1918. Indeed, for some time it was barely clear that there was a problem at all. Not only was the country stretched and battered by war, but death from infectious disease was far more common in those days: bronchitis, measles, scarlet fever and tuberculosis were all regular killers.† The flu was not mentioned in Parliament until October 1918, well into the second wave, and was only made notifiable to the

---

* Technically not a Zeppelin: his victim was SL-11, a wooden-framed airship built by Schütte-Lanz, as opposed to the metal-framed Zeppelins. Some fragments of this airship are on display at the Bletchley Park code-breaking museum.

† This may also help explain why, at least until COVID-19, Spanish flu had rather been forgotten by history. 'Only' flu, no matter how serious, can seem mild when set against the trauma of war. The fatality rate was still small when compared with the number of cases, and the timing also saw it conflated into the overall war experience.

authorities when the third wave hit in early 1919. And even then there was no coherent strategy for dealing with it: no National Health Service, of course, not for another 30 years, and the central board of health could only advise local authorities what to do rather than instruct them. Into the vacuum came a predictable troupe of chancers, quacks, charlatans and folk remedies: Dr Williams's Pink Pills for Pale People, Veno's Lightning Cough Cure, Thompson's Influenza Specific ('acts like magic!'), eating raw onions and drinking whisky (not necessarily together). And churches were kept open rather than being closed, as they were during the first wave of COVID-19, on the grounds that people would need religion and faith more than ever at this time.

COVID-19: SOME EARLY FINDINGS

The very sudden onset of the coronavirus pandemic posed the ONS a number of challenges in measuring it, and doing so rapidly enough to be useful in formulating a policy response. This went further than simply counting how many people were dying from it – grim but necessary statistics though those were – but the regular figure of weekly deaths in England and Wales went from one of the least noticed figures that the statisticians produce to being, at the height of the lockdown, perhaps their most closely studied and widely reported data series. Meanwhile, the number of people who were clicking into the blogs that the ONS posted to help explain how these figures were derived and what they meant showed a real hunger among the public for trusted information on what was happening all around them.* Naturally people wanted to know how many of the deaths reported every week were from the pandemic, and so the ONS rapidly began to publish separate analysis on how many registered deaths had COVID-19 mentioned on the certificate, and also looked at the number of 'excess deaths' – that is, the extent to which the number of deaths during the height of the infection was above what might be expected for that time of year anyway.

While the records of those who died give an idea of the scale of the Spanish flu, for the latest pandemic we

---

* The watchdog for official statistics, the United Kingdom Statistics Authority, regularly tracks public trust in official statistics. It's too early to say how COVID-19 has affected this, but the most recent figures, published in March 2019, showed that 85 per cent of those who expressed an opinion trusted ONS figures.

also have evidence for its spread in the community, as the ONS, with a number of partner organisations, was asked to set up a survey to measure precisely that. Of course, not everyone who is infected with COVID-19 develops symptoms, and these people may well not seek a test. So it was necessary to select households at random and, with their co-operation, visit them at home to carry out tests. Recent results of the survey showed that, in the week ending 15 January 2022, during the spike caused by the Omicron variant, there were an estimated 3 million people in England alone with COVID-19, up from 148,000 between 27 April and 10 May 2020 in the first wave of the pandemic. In order for it be useful, all this had to be set up in far, far less time than is normally the case with a new survey – indeed, the establishment of the survey was announced by the ONS in late April 2020, less than a month after the onset of the lockdown, with the first results published barely three weeks after that.

Another difference between 1918–19 and the latest global pandemic is that we are much more able to adopt precautionary measures to reduce the risk of transmission, whether by working from home or ordering what we need over the internet. Many jobs, of course, can't be done remotely, or aren't needed for the time being if the whole business is closed to the public – but these days many can. Moreover, how well were members of the public adhering to the new rules and government advice? All that needed measurement. A new online survey from the ONS found that, in April 2020, at the height of the lockdown, just under half of all those in employment (46.6 per cent, to be precise) did at least some work from home, and overwhelmingly (86.0 per cent) the reason for this was because of the pandemic. It was particularly people in white-collar occupations who were able to do this: managers, directors and senior officials, professional occupations and associate professional and technical occupations all saw homeworking rates of around two-thirds, and getting on for three-fifths of administrative and secretarial occupations also worked at home. By contrast, all other occupations saw less than one-fifth of staff working from home. Likewise, in May 2020, when non-essential shops were still closed, the total value of retail sales was almost 10 per cent lower than it had been in the same month of 2019 but, within this, internet sales were up hugely: 57.9 per cent higher than in May 2019, to be precise. As at December 2021, internet sales values remained 36 per cent higher than two years earlier, before the pandemic.

We also know a good deal about how people felt and reacted to this pandemic and went along with the lockdown measures, thanks to the Opinions and Lifestyle Survey from the ONS. Soon after the lockdown was imposed, for example, between 27 March and 6 April 2020, the proportion of people who said they were 'very' or 'somewhat' worried about the effect of COVID-19 on their life right now was 84.2 per cent; but this gradually declined, and by 25 to 28 June, it was down to 68.6 per cent – though that's still more than two in every three people, of course. The survey also asked people whether they had stuck to the lockdown. In the period 3 to 13 April, for example, 85 per cent of adults in Great Britain said that in the past week they had stayed at home or only left for the four permitted reasons.* That proportion didn't decline very much until the government began to ease the lockdown in England in mid-May. Meanwhile, around the start of the lockdown, 89.8 per cent of people said they were washing their hands more often than previously (no-one was claiming to be doing *less* handwashing). This survey has continued to

---

* Just in case you've forgotten already: work, exercise, essential shopping or medical needs.

monitor people's behaviour, showing that in the period 15 December 2021 to 3 January 2022, for example, 57 per cent of adults said they had taken a rapid lateral flow test in the past seven days, up from 42 per cent in the previous fortnight.

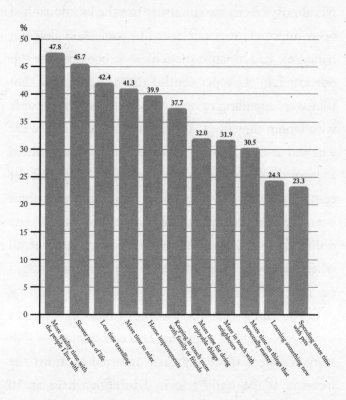

Figure 27: Some of the lifestyle benefits reported from the COVID-19 pandemic
Source: Office for National Statistics

And let's not forget that every cloud has, proverbially, a silver lining: to set against the toll on human life and the economic damage wrought by the pandemic, the survey shows that it has also brought some positive reactions. In the period 25 to 28 June 2020, for example, almost exactly two months after the lockdown had been imposed, 46.8 per cent of people said that the pandemic had brought them lifestyle benefits. The top one cited, by 47.8 per cent of those people, was that they were spending more quality time with the people with whom they lived. Those who are convinced we're a nation of animal lovers, however, will be disappointed to learn that less than half this number – only 23.3 per cent – said they were spending more time with their pets. Generally, people thought that they would keep doing these things after the pandemic, most of all when it came to those who were exercising more (91.5 per cent of them).

If you think that these sorts of facts and figures sound familiar, that might not be a coincidence – ONS statistics were quite regularly referred to from the lecterns at the daily televised briefings held at 10 Downing Street. As at early 2022 it seems still safe to say that the effects of this pandemic will be with us for a long while yet. It is surely still too soon to be sure

how much of what has changed has changed for ever
(will nine in 10 of us really keep up our extra exercise?)
but we can be confident that the official figures will be
there to help us figure it all out.

PART FIVE

2121:
BACK TO
THE FUTURE?

One of the most striking things about the history of the census is that it has coincided more or less exactly with the most rapid and seismic period of social, economic and political change in British history. For many centuries, the fundamentals of British life changed very slowly, if at all. A time traveller plucked from the Battle of Hastings in 1066 and set down in the London of six centuries later, on the eve of the Great Fire, would have found little to surprise him: more people, to be sure, and a greater sophistication in building materials and techniques, but otherwise more or less unchanged in terms of transport (horses and boats), government (monarchical rule, the recently ended Protectorate notwithstanding) and employment (agriculture, trade and cottage industries).

Now reduce that time gap by a factor of three, from 600 years to 200 years. Put a traveller from 1666 down in 1866 and he would have found much more to surprise him, with the Industrial Revolution having transformed parts of the country, and the cities it spawned growing and sprawling almost like living organisms. Now halve the gap again, from 1866 to 1966, and the difference would be twice as noticeable, despite the shorter time span: cars, planes, telephones, televisions. Another halving of the gap from 1966 to 2016, and a world dominated by an internet that hadn't even been thought of back then; already it looks as though the internet will be the technology that defines the early twenty-first century just as much as the coal-fired steam engine did the nineteenth and the internal combustion engine the twentieth.

The pace of change continues not just to accelerate but to do so exponentially. So, having examined the 1921 census as a one-of-a-kind snapshot, due to the effects of the First World War and Spanish flu, and knowing that the 2021 census, when the results start coming out shortly, will also in some way reflect the coronavirus pandemic, it is interesting to look ahead as best we can to what a 2121 census might look like. As the American baseball player and coach Yogi Berra once opined, 'It's tough to make predictions, especially about the future', and any attempts to foresee a century hence are fraught with inaccuracies so vast as to be unknowable. Two things can, however, be said with certainty: that many aspects of society will be more or less unrecognisable, but also that much of what we think will change may not do so, and vice versa. Look at how many predictions of our age involved flying cars, for example. Indeed, 38 years after George Orwell's bleak vision of the future was set, one can argue that even the bits of it that have come true haven't done so at all in the ways he was expecting. And of course the date when *Blade Runner* is set is already more than two years past, but Los Angeles has yet to be overrun by replicants. Moreover, when it comes to how the official data of the future will be collected and analysed, while it seems certain that there will be huge technological changes – though exactly what is definitely unpredictable – there will surely be some fundamental principles that won't have changed, and to conclude this part and indeed the book as a whole, let's take a look at what those might be.

So, with those caveats firmly in place, here's a dispatch from the frontline of 2121:

CENSUS 2121

Welcome to the executive summary of Census 2121, which comes free of charge straight to your personal nanobot information interface implant and is optimised for all operating systems. Hard copies can be purchased by organisations and individuals who wish, but users are reminded that this outmoded method of communication does not update in real time.

In times past, censuses were taken every 10 years, and acted as national snapshots in order to help governments formulate policy and allocate resources. In the nineteenth century, these decennial revisitings were more or less the only nationwide registers available. Gradually things began to change, and by the late twentieth and early twenty-first centuries, the Office for National Statistics was compiling figures on a regular basis across all sectors of society and the economy, permitting a much more accurate and easily updatable picture of the nation than had previously been available.

Yet it is axiomatic that one generation's advance is the next generation's anachronism. From this distance, figures collated quarterly or even monthly seem positively prehistoric with regards to our society, where universal and perfectly accurate information is available up not just to the second but the nanosecond. In retrospect, the shift away from the traditional methods began with the 2021 census, which was hailed as the first to be 'digital first' – though it employed what now seems the unbelievably primitive technology of the 'internet', which was made obsolete by the development of the Global Telepathy Network.

The current Hive OS XXXII, the latest iteration of the Global Telepathy Network, is faster and more reliable than ever before. In effect, the census now is perpetual, constantly updating itself. But, for the sake of tradition and statistical continuity, an official census statement is still produced every 10 years at a given moment. So, as of 21.21 hours and 21 seconds on 21 February 2121, the vital statistics for the United Kingdom are as follows.

WHO WE ARE

The population of the UK is 82,488,384. For the first time at any decennial census point, the number of centenarians in the country has passed the 400,000 mark. (The 400,000th centenarian was actually recorded on 21 February 2117, an event marked by a virtual audience with King George VII, who himself attained his century on 22 July 2113, becoming the UK's first monarch to do so), and the number now stands at 423,110. By way of contrast, there were only 16,715 centenarians in the UK 100 years ago in 2021.

Increased life expectancy, together with net migration, accounts for the increasing national population. The fertility rate has remained more or less steady, between 1.7 and 1.8, for many decades now. There were 801,603 live births in 2120, of which 272,572 (34 per cent) came via ectogenesis, artificial wombs that negate the need for mothers to undergo nine months of uncomfortable and possibly painful pregnancy. As those figures show, however, almost two-thirds of mothers still prefer to give birth the 'natural' way, citing as their main reasons the connection to their inherent biology and desire to bond with the baby pre-birth (48 per cent), tradition and a link to the past (27 per cent), distrust of the ectogenetic process (21 per cent)* and religious objections (4 per cent).

Fewer than 20 per cent of the population remain completely biologically human: that is, without any form of machine augmentation or prosthesis in their brains and/or bodies. The rights of these people – known as 'naturals' by themselves and 'Luddites'† by their critics – were enshrined in the Protection of Humanity Act 2048, as amended in 2066, 2091 and 2112. Brain augmentation through neural interface is the most popular form of transhuman‡ modification (88.2 per cent), followed by

---

* Distrust of the ectogenetic process may seem bizarre and misplaced, given that by definition it is engineered to be foolproof and failsafe, and that its success rate has been 100 per cent ever since inadequate safety precautions were overhauled in the wake of the 2076 Wildflower Clinic scandal. But fear of scientific processes has long been a human trait that no amount of technological advance can seemingly totally eradicate: 100 years ago, strange as this seems to us, many people were terrified of flying.

† The Luddites were originally a secret organisation of nineteenth-century English textile workers who destroyed machinery in protest at the perceived threat to their jobs. The term was gradually expanded to mean anyone opposed to industrialisation, automation, computerisation or new technologies in general.

‡ The earlier term 'cyborg' failed to catch on, mainly as a result of negative connotations deriving from old science fiction.

gene editing (81.9 per cent), robotic/cybernetic skeleto-muscular enhancements (74.2 per cent), artificial organs (69.4 per cent) and synthetic blood (26.7 per cent).

Just over two-fifths of adults (40.4 per cent) are married or in RCPs (Renewable Civil Partnerships). Of these, only 12 per cent have chosen to marry 'till death do us part'. Greater life expectancy has led to increasing numbers of people seeking RCPs, where both parties are obliged to recommit at regular intervals: five years is most common (56 per cent), followed by 10 years (24 per cent) and three years (12 per cent); thus effectively enforcing an opt-in rather than opt-out system. A little more than a third (34.6 per cent) are single.

Speculation in the early part of the twenty-first century that white Britons would become an ethnic minority by the end of that century – the first time in history that a major indigenous population had voluntarily become a minority, rather than through war, famine or disease – have not come to pass. Just over 80 per cent of the 2021 population was classified as white British, a figure which is now 65.7 per cent.

Despite the nation's increasing ethnic diversity, 95.2 per cent of people now speak English as a first language. This is very much in line with global trends, where the 'Big Three' languages – English, Spanish and Mandarin –

are between them spoken by more than 90 per cent of the world's population. For a while in the twenty-first century, it seemed that instantaneous electronic translation programs would permit the preservation of languages across the world, but in fact they had the opposite effect and led to increasing linguistic hegemony. Many European, Asian and African languages have now died out entirely, or are kept alive by only a handful of scholars.

Only 9.7 per cent of the population now class themselves as 'religious' in any form whatsoever. Technical and scientific advances have become so commonplace, and yet from the point of view of our ancestors so extraordinary, that for many people the German philosopher Friedrich Nietzsche's 'God is dead' tenet has finally come true. Even many of those who declare themselves religious are more so 'culturally' rather than literally (that is, as in believing the infallibility or sanctity of texts hitherto thought sacred).

An even smaller amount – 8.0 per cent – took a physical holiday in 2120. Travel for leisure is now a minority interest for the very rich, much as it was in the days of the 'Grand Tour' and even into the nineteenth century. More than 75 per cent of people think that leisure travel is morally wrong, citing environmental damage and exploitation of local culture as their main reasons. In contrast, 87.1 per cent of people took a virtual holiday last year, using one or more of the main three VVR (Virtual Vacation Reality) programs to recreate in hyper-realistic detail the sights, sounds, smells and itineraries of the holidays enjoyed in yesteryear. The most popular form of virtual holiday was a beach vacation (65.8 per cent), followed by adventure vacations (62 per cent), city breaks (55.9 per cent) and cruises (46.3 per cent). One exception to the trend towards to VVR is *Love Island*, the longest-running infoscreen download, and almost the only one surviving from the days of the old 'television' technology. Now past 200 series, it is still filmed in an actual location.

Eating real meat or fish is now as exclusive, expensive and controversial as taking real vacations. Only 7.7 per cent of people ate real meat or fish at all in 2120; small wonder, perhaps, with a kilo of steak costing an average of RP1250 and a kilo of salmon RP1890.* 57.2 per cent

* The Ripple (RP) digital settlement system is now as near to global standard as makes no difference, and is certainly used throughout the UK as the one and only legal tender. Fiat currency, interest rates and exchange trading were all eliminated under the terms of the 2045 Vancouver Protocol. Banknotes and coins are collectors' curiosities.

of people are totally vegan (this can include eating artificial meat made from vegetable products), with 27.1 per cent also eating cultured meat or fish (grown in laboratories but involving no harm to actual animals) and 8.0 per cent identifying as the old definition of vegetarianism (prepared to eat eggs and dairy products).

WHAT WE DO

The short answer to this is 'much less than our ancestors'. The average male employee works 19 hours per week and the average female 17, less than half the amount their counterparts did in 2021, when the average man worked 37 and the average woman 34.

This is, of course, due to the rise not so much of mass automation – that was already in place for many processes 100 years ago – but of mass *smart* automation, greatly increasing the breadth and depth of areas in which machines can take the place of humans or transhumans. In the nineteenth century, British manufacturing was the most advanced in the world. By 2021, it represented less than 10 per cent of employment. By the mid-twenty-first century, traditional manufacturing had declined to negligible levels. The rise of 3-D printers and nanofabricators meant that production became increasingly decentralised: people could make almost anything at home rather than needing to buy it fully fabricated. This revolution in manufacturing, combined with the exponential growth in computer intelligence, changed the nature of work itself throughout the mid- to late-twenty-first century.

It was not just the menial and unskilled or semi-skilled jobs that became automated during this time, but also the ones that our ancestors regarded as skilled: much of a doctor's, lawyer's or banker's work was taken over by smart robots during that time too. All this fed into a gradual cultural shift, moving away from the central place of work (and overwork) in people's lives and towards a greater emphasis on leisure, free time and creativity.

98.9 per cent of the population have some form of contact with robots in their daily lives. There are 32.6 million personal robots,* 28.17 million professional

---

* These include kitchen chefs, lawnmowers, personal mobility assistants, pet exercise robots, toys and vacuum cleaners.

service robots* and 2.54 million industrial robots† in the UK today.

Ten jobs that exist now which didn't exist in 2021:

1. Body-part maker, in charge of growing and maintaining spare organs or parts of organs to allow easy replacement (and obviate the need for organ donors).

2. Weather control technician, to mitigate the effects of extreme weather events (making it rain in cases of drought, diverting paths of tornadoes and so on). Still restricted very much to government circles as much by the sheer cost of the technology as by the complexity of regulatory issues.

3. Space junk disposal expert, collecting and disposing of debris left in earth's orbit, mostly from old satellites but also some coming from more modern spaceships.

* These include automated security patrols, delivery robots, fire-fighting robots, medical robots, public cleaning robots and retail assistance robots.

† These are for larger-scale manufacturing, itself largely superseded, and are therefore much less numerous than the other two categories.

4. Space pilot, taking tourists into space and running shuttle flights to the Moon (now partially terraformed and permanently inhabited since 2069, the centenary of the first lunar landing by Apollo 11).

5. Wine grower. Of course, there was a British wine industry in 2021, but not to the same extent as today, as climate change has rendered the UK much more suitable for climate grape varieties such as Sangiovese, Cabernet Sauvignon and Grenache.

6. Vertical farmer, working on vertical farms ('farmscrapers') in cities (see 'Where We Live').

7. Memory augmentation surgeon, inserting and maintaining neural meshes and quantum chip implants.

8. AI psychologist, helping maintain the 'mental' and 'emotional' equilibrium of ever more advanced and self-learning artificial intelligence. AI psychologists need to understand both psychology and technology in equal measures.

9. Quantum data analyst, measuring quantum information and helping businesses maintain 'perfect' quantum level encryption.

10. Soft-skill consultant, teaching people to maximise their 'soft skills' (oral communication, leadership, time management and so on) in order to differentiate them from machine technology.

Ten jobs that existed in 2021 which no longer exist:

1. Chauffeur and taxi driver. All vehicles are now self-driving, though of course a few diehards still like to keep their classic mid-twenty-first-century electrics on the road as a hobby.

2. Pilot. As with drivers, planes are now entirely automated.

3. Shopping mall worker. Vast shopping centres died out with the advent of 3-D printers and increasing tendencies toward online purchasing.

4. Travel agent. The demise of the travel industry has meant that old-fashioned travel agents simply ceased to exist. Those wealthy enough to afford travel nowadays tend to have their arrangements made by the specialist concierge services that cater for all aspects of their life.

5. Cashier. Even in 2021 this was a diminishing sector, with an increasing number of self-service tills and ever greater reliance on bank cards rather than cash. The last human cashier was phased out in 2046.

6. Librarian. Mainly because there are no libraries left either, bar the five copyright libraries, which are now museums and archives rather than libraries. All mainstream books have been electronic for decades

now, though again a small number of traditionalists like to hang on to their collection of old paper books, despite the frustrating inability of these to update in real time.

7. Postal worker. Postmen and -women used to bring letters, cards, bills and statements to houses across the country on a daily basis. All these forms of communication have long been electronic.

8. Textile worker. Clothes design is still human work, but the actual manufacturing is all automated.

9. Sports referee/umpire. Technology is now infallible and available in real time, ensuring that decisions are always correct. However, predictions that this would prevent sports fans claiming that the refbot's video input must be 'on the blink'* unfortunately proved unfounded.

10. Lumberjack. Wood and trees are now protected from any kind of commercial exploitation, with new buildings made from technology unimaginable in 2021.

---

* This old expression for some machine being faulty probably derives from the tendency of early televisions – a twentieth-century precursor to modern infoscreens – to begin flickering when they were starting to go wrong.

WHERE WE LIVE

More than 98 per cent of the population live in areas that are 'irreversibly built-up in character': that is, villages, towns and cities. With more people has come more housing, turning villages into towns and towns into cities.

All the main urban areas have grown in size over the last century. Greater London, as now delineated, is home to 12.7 million people, though of course the wider urban area extends across much more of south-east England than it did in 2021. The LiverMan urban area, comprising the former cities of Liverpool and Manchester, which became one unbroken urban conglomeration in 2076, has a population of 4.9 million. West Midlands is now 4.1 million in size, and West Yorkshire 3.2 million. After these comes Solentside, the conurbation that has swallowed up Bournemouth, Poole, Portsmouth and Southampton and which now totals 2.8 million people.

Just prior to the 2021 period (when the level was artificially low because of a global pandemic), almost a million and half people used the London Underground system every year. Despite the increase in the city's population, that figure has now fallen to below 1 billion, with the fall in demand caused by the sharply decreasing numbers of 'commuters' (people who regularly travelled to a workplace physically distant from their homes) and the system finding it difficult to cope with the increasingly extreme climate (London, a massive heat island, is on average three degrees warmer than the rest of the country). As a result, the 'Tube' system has become a seasonal railway: a metro stopping service in winter and a quasi-express line for a limited number of stations in summer. Remaining commuters are encouraged to use the automated vehicle system above ground or to get around on foot.

The climate has encouraged a greater sense of demarcation between regions. Southern England is now as hot as the Mediterranean was in the early twenty-first century, and residents there have adopted what was widely seen as a traditional Mediterranean lifestyle: an outdoor culture, siestas in the afternoon and going out to eat late in the evening. In contrast, northern England and particularly Scotland still maintain a reasonably temperate climate (though clearly much warmer than a century before) and therefore a lifestyle that would, in strictly climatic terms, be more or less recognisable to dwellers from the previous century.

Across the nation, there are more than 20 farmscrapers: tower blocks with crops stacked on top of each other, like the floors of a building. With space at a premium, an urban footprint of just 1.32 hectares can produce the same quantity of food as 420 hectares of conventional farming. The enclosed and tightly controlled farmscraper environment particularly suits genetically modified crops, and food can be sold in the same place as it's grown.

2,379 UK citizens are currently living on the Moon, and 528 are posted to the recently built international research station on Mars.

CONCLUSION

Will we have lunar settlements, transhumans and farmscrapers by 2121? Obviously we can't know these sorts of things (though it seems a safe bet that even if Merseyside and Greater Manchester have fused into one giant settlement, the different districts thereof will be passionate supporters of different teams in whatever is the twenty-second century's most popular sport), and no doubt I've given some pretty big hostages to fortune in my prognostications. But one thing seems certain: that however they will do it, our descendants a century on will still have a need to measure the key things in their life by putting numbers on them, for, going back to Lord Kelvin's dictum, 'if you cannot measure it, you cannot improve it'. And though the methods of producing these statistics will surely change and be updated at the very least as much in the next 100 years as they have in the last, one thing that won't change is the vital role of official statistics in measuring the country and thus letting us improve it. How will those statistics be collected and disseminated?

One thing that will be clear to the diligent reader is that the administrative arrangements for collecting data are changeable. From the commissioners of William the Conqueror, sent to collect the Domesday Book records, through the various Poor Law overseers, teachers and tax collectors sent out to take early censuses in the UK, through the Central Statistical Office and the Office of Population Censuses and Surveys of the post-war years, to today's Office for National Statistics, the administrative arrangements have altered down the years. Likewise, at one time the post of national statistician was also combined with that of registrar general for England and Wales, but in 2008 the latter job came under the remit of HM Passport Office instead. What happens in the future is uncertain, but there will surely be a challenge for the producers of official statistics in making sure that they can keep abreast of private interests, such as big social media or retail platforms, which routinely gather vast quantities of information about their users. The challenge for organisations like the ONS, and its opposite numbers in different countries, will surely be to try to make sure that policymakers and citizens can know at least as much about their populations and economies as the internet behemoths. Moreover, the UK Statistics Authority – to which the ONS answers – only looked ahead five years in its 2020 strategy. The key aims here include: building public trust in evidence; making data available in a secure way for research and evaluation; enhancing understanding of social, economic and environmental matters; and improving clarity and coherence of communication for maximum impact. But these key objectives – however they may have been reformulated in the words of the day – will surely still be valid in a hundred years' time. With that in mind, let's try to make a few predictions about the future of official statistics.

More data will be gathered in real time in the future, which will enable quicker results and less reliance on surveys, with their inherent sampling variability. The ONS is already moving towards this in a number of areas, and the onset of the coronavirus pandemic showed how useful some of these indicators could be at a time when there was a real need for faster data. For example, work was already being done on price data automatically 'scraped' from retailers' websites. At the start of the lockdown, when many items, such as long-life food, toilet rolls and hand sanitiser, became hard to find in shops, this information was used to monitor how prices in these areas were moving, gathering information on a daily basis – this showed, for example, that while the price of kitchen rolls rose slightly in late March 2020, it rapidly declined thereafter and by mid-July they were actually 5 per cent cheaper than at the start of the pandemic. Likewise, the existing survey on job vacancies was supplemented by faster data on online job adverts, which pointed to the decline in vacancies bottoming out a couple of months into the lockdown before the survey results confirmed this and was, as I write, suggesting that in early 2022 the huge bounceback of late 2021 was petering out. How exactly similar things will be done in the future depends in large part on future technologies, but one thing we can be sure of: we'll be seeing official data on many aspects of life faster than we do now.

There has, in the past, been talk about moving away from the decennial census in its traditional form, and indeed, after 2011, the ONS did consult on whether another one was needed (the recommendation, of course, was that, yes, a 2021 census should be held, in an online-first approach). Thereafter, the question is more open: after 2021 the question will be looked at again, with recommendations due to be delivered in 2023. The aim of this would be to see whether administrative data, such as information from sources such as the Ordnance Survey, GP registrations and driving licence details, combined with population surveys, could replace the census more cheaply. Moreover, of course, because the census only happens once every ten years, over time the value of the data to decision-makers decreases, until another census becomes available ten years down the road (though, even so, during the pandemic, the 2011 figures have proved in great demand, with ONS census staff working flat out to meet data requests from the Cabinet Office and other government departments and from collaborative groups of researchers from various universities and institutions).

However, the current national statistician has made it clear that the ONS would only recommend moving away from the census if the richness of data it could provide could be replicated in other ways. Indeed, so much has the census become one of the institutions of British life that the mere suggestion that it might not continue was enough to spark coverage on the BBC, both on *The World at One* and even a phone-in with Jeremy Vine. However, one thing is clear: the country will continue to need to gather the key baseline data, such as how many people there are in the country and whereabouts they live, whether or not that is done via a traditional census.

Once gathered, however that is done, the security of personal data and its proper collection and use will surely remain paramount. As the ability to link different datasets grows, new things will become possible – the ONS has, for example, already used anonymised data from the 2011 census with attainment records from the National Pupil Database to look at how children's home lives can shape their educational attainment. But this sort of research using very personal data needs to be done responsibly. Naturally, everyone has a right to privacy and to have their personal data protected. It is hard to see it ever being acceptable to the public, even a hundred years hence, that the country's official number-crunchers should not take the greatest care with their data, and it is also important that new ways of collecting data should be properly thought through. For example, even something as seemingly innocuous as the way ONS collects price data from retailers' public-facing websites is subject to the rules it has implemented.* Some sort of framework to govern the ethical conduct of all this will surely continue, even if does not take the exact same form as at present with the National Statistician's Data Ethics Advisory Committee.

If you've got this far with this book, that probably means you're not one of those people who implicitly distrusts all official statistics; and you're in good company if so. The UK Statistics Authority regularly monitors public trust in ONS data; and as already noted its most recent survey, published early in 2019, found that, of those who had an opinion on the matter, 85 per cent trusted ONS data. No matter whether this number will have risen or fallen in the future, it will be vital to maintaining trust that official statistics are well communicated to the general public – who, after all, pay for the system through their taxes. New technologies will provide new ways of doing this – just as first the internet and then the rise of social media already have – but, while they may replace old means of distributing figures, such as the fax-back service the

---

* For example, the programs are set up to do this at times of day when other traffic to those websites are likely to be at their lowest, so as to minimise the risk of accidental disruption.

ONS press office used to provide for the latest economic data, they will not do away with the need for clear explanation.

The Scottish poet and critic Andrew Lang famously accused politicians of using statistics in the same way that a drunk uses lamp-posts – 'for support rather than illumination'. In this book, I've been trying to throw an affectionate spotlight on what the data tell us about who we are, what we do and where we live. I'll leave it up to you to decide whether you have been illuminated by all this; but I hope you do now, if you didn't already, understand a little about the importance of being able to put a yardstick up alongside the country we live in.

SOURCES

Online sources

Most of the statistics were sourced from the Office for National Statistics (ONS) website: **www.ons.gov.uk**.

Other websites used include:

1911census.org – **www.1911census.org.uk**

BBC – **www.bbc.co.uk**

BBC History Extra – **www.historyextra.com**

British Library – **www.bl.uk**

Economic History Association – **https://eh.net**

Financial Times – **www.ft.com**

Guardian – **www.theguardian.com**

GOV.UK – **www.gov.uk**

Historic Accommodation Guide – **www.historic-uk. com/AccommodationGuide/**

History of Government blog
  – https://history.blog.gov.uk
The National Archives
  – www.nationalarchives.gov.uk
Parliament – www.parliament.uk
Prospect magazine – www.prospectmagazine.co.uk
Rootsweb.com – http://rootsweb.com
Striking Women – www.striking-women.org
UK Census Online – https://ukcensusonline.com
UK Data Service – http://ukdataservice.ac.uk
University of Cambridge – www.cam.ac.uk
University of Oxford, Faculty of History
  – www.history.ox.ac.uk
Victorianchildren.org – https://victorianchildren.org
VisitBritain – www.visitbritain.org

Printed Sources

Department of Employment and Productivity, *British Labour Statistics: Historical Abstract 1886–1968* (London, HMSO, 1971).

Howlett, Peter, *Fighting with Figures: a Statistical Digest of the Second World War* (London: HMSO, 1995).

Hutchinson, Roger, *The Butcher, the Baker, the Candlestick-Maker: The Story of Britain through its*

Census, since 1801 (London: Little, Brown, 2017).

Merry, Emma, with support from Kay Callaghan and Chris Cotton, *First Names: the Definitive Guide to Popular Names in England and Wales 1944–1994 and in the Regions 1994* (London: HMSO, 1995).

Nissel, Muriel, *People Count: A History of the General Register Office* (London: HMSO, 1987).

Ward, Reg, and Doggett, Ted, *Keeping Score: the First Fifty Years of the Central Statistical Office* (London: HMSO, 1991).

RESOURCES AND FURTHER READING

There are so many resources online for those who wish to find out more about official statistics that this can be only a cursory glance at what is available at the time of writing.

The ONS website, **www.ons.gov.uk**, is its main repository for current statistical releases, as well as related information and corporate announcements. Older statistical releases have been moved to The National Archives website: **https://webarchive. nationalarchives.gov.uk/20160105160709/ http://www.ons.gov.uk/ons/index.html**. ONS contact details for public enquiries can be found on the website **https://www.ons.gov.uk/aboutus/contactus/ generalandstatisticalenquiries** (for historical census queries, though, see ONS Census Customer Services below). You can follow the ONS via social media on

Twitter at **www.twitter.com/ONS**, on LinkedIn at **www.linkedin.com/company/office-for-national-statistics** and on Facebook at **www.facebook.com/ONS**. The ONS also produces a blog, *National Statistical*, which covers statistical developments across the Office generally: **https://blog.ons.gov.uk/**. Another Twitter account, **www.twitter.com/onsfocus**, is the place to follow all the latest news about the ONS itself.

There is a dedicated website for the 2021 census in England and Wales: **https://census.gov.uk/**. In addition, you can follow the census on Twitter (in English, **www.twitter.com/census2021** and Welsh, **www.twitter.com/Cyfrifiad2021**) and Facebook (English, **www.facebook.com/census2021/** and Welsh, **www.facebook.com/Cyfrifiad2021**). For information on the 2021 census in Northern Ireland, see **www.nisra.gov.uk/statistics/census/2021-census** and for the Scottish census, see **www.scotlandscensus.gov.uk/**.

Our Census Customer Services team provides expert advice about the 2011 Census and earlier censuses. It can be contacted on (0)1329 444972 or **census.customerservices@ons.gov.uk**.

There is also a website covering the work of the ONS Data Science Campus, **https://datascience**

campus.ons.gov.uk/, and you can follow the DSC on Twitter at **www.twitter.com/DataSciCampus**.

The United Kingdom Statistics Authority, of which the ONS is the executive office, is an independent body at arm's length from government. It has a statutory objective of promoting and safeguarding the production and publication of official statistics that serve the public good, and its website is at **www.statisticsauthority.gov.uk**. The Office for Statistics Regulation is the regulatory arm of the UK Statistics Authority. It assesses official statistics for compliance with the Code of Practice for Statistics, reports on system-wide issues and on how statistics are used. Its website is **https://osr.statisticsauthority.gov.uk**.

Many official statistics from other government departments are published on the GOV.UK website, and can be found here: **www.gov.uk/search/research-and-statistics**.

A very useful resource for a number of ONS data series, including labour-market surveys, business surveys, births, marriages and also censuses back to that of 1981, is the Nomis website at **www.nomisweb.co.uk**.

UK data for the Sustainable Development Goals can be found at **https://sdgdata.gov.uk/**. The

ONS publishes a dashboard on its well-being indicators at www.ons.gov.uk/peoplepopulationandcommunity/wellbeing/articles/measuresofnationalwellbeing dashboard/2018-04-25.

For advice on looking at old census records, there is a guide on The National Archives website at www.nationalarchives.gov.uk/help-with-your research/research-guides/census-records/.

ACKNOWLEDGEMENTS

Boris Starling

I would like to thank David Bradbury of the ONS for his assistance in finding statistics and Joel Simons and Sarah Hammond of HarperCollins for all their help in putting this book together.

David Bradbury of the Office for National Statistics

There are a number of debts I ought to acknowledge. Firstly, I would like to thank both Boris Starling and the team at HarperCollins for being such excellent collaborators, the difficulties of working together amid lockdown notwithstanding. I would also like to thank the various statisticians in ONS and elsewhere who helped me to find long-run data or who answered my various queries. Finally, I must thank my colleagues in the ONS media relations office for their collective forbearance for the time I devoted to this project at what was an exceptionally busy time for all of us, not least our head of press, Miles Fletcher, for his support in seeing this all through to fruition.

INDEX

Page references in *italics* denote figures and tables; n denotes a note.

INDEX

Craddock, Dr, 104n
crossing sweepers, 148
cyber security, 155

Dallas (TV series), 61
data analysts, 156
database administrators, 156
David, King of Israel and
    Judah, 8
Davison, Emily, 23
death
  annual rates, decrease in,
    117–18
  COVID-19, 238, 245
  and disease, 118, 122–3
  in First World War, 233–4
  industrial accidents, 135,
    177–8, *179*
  motor vehicle crashes, 119
  recording of, 2
  Spanish flu, 237–8
  and time of year, 124
  unusual causes, 119–22
  see also life expectancy
delivery drivers and couriers,
    156
Department of Employment,
    26
Department for Work and
    Pensions, 117
Derbyshire, 208n

disease
  cholera, 230
  fatal, change in, 119
  post-First World War, 243
  smallpox, 73, 230
  urbanisation, 186
  see also COVID-19;
    Spanish flu pandemic
Disraeli, Benjamin:
    Coningsby, 194
divorce, 68, 130
dog walkers, 157
Domesday Book, 2, 10–12,
    14, 276
domestic service, 138, *139*,
    158, 162, 189
Dorset County Council,
    100n
Dover, 80
Driscoll, Bridget, 121
driving licences, 279
drug use, 218
Dubai, 108
Dumfries, 208n

earnings, *see* wages
East Anglia, 189
Eastbourne, 196
education
  and automation, 171
  budgets, 101

INDEX